BECOMING STRESS-RESISTANT
Through the Project SMART Program

Raymond B. Flannery, Jr., Ph.D.

CHEVRON
PUBLISHING CORPORATION

2003
Chevron Publishing Corporation
5018 Dorsey Hall Drive, Suite 104
Ellicott City, MD 21042
(410) 740-0065

1994
The Crossroad Publishing Company
370 Lexington Avenue
New York, NY 10017

1990
The Continuum Publishing Company
370 Lexington Avenue
New York, NY 10017

Printed in the United States of America.

ISBN: 1-883581-37-0

For My Wife Georgina

CONTENTS

Also by Raymond B. Flannery, Jr., Ph.D.

Posttraumatic Stress Disorder:
The Victim's Guide to Healing and Recovery

Violence in the Workplace

The Assaulted Staff Action Program (ASAP):
Coping with the Psychological Aftermath of Violence

Violence in America:
Coping with Drugs, Distressed Families,
Inadequate Schooling, and Acts of Hate

Preventing Youth Violence:
A Guide for Parents, Teachers, and Counselors

Preface to the Chevron Edition

Becoming Stress-Resistant was first published in December 1990. Since then the country has been through the Gulf war, the Balkans conflict, the Afghanistan war, and the Iraq war. These years also saw the 9/11 World Trade Center attack, the rise of terrorism worldwide, the shootings at Columbine and several other high schools, and several national and man-made disasters, including the NASA space shuttle, Columbia. The national economy failed, some major corporations were shown to be corrupt, and a global economic downturn ensued. For many, both immediate income and future retirement plans were uprooted. Add to these major stressful events the basic life tasks of obtaining an education, career development, finding a significant other, rearing a family, taking care of one's aging parents, and planning for retirement. It is no wonder that many of us experience time scarcity, a sense of loss of control, and continuing emotional distress. Road rage should not surprise us.

As bad as this currently is, it is likely to get worse. Computers, a central force in today's age, currently run on nanoseconds (one billion times faster than a human second). The next generation of computers to come online will run on pico seconds (one trillion times faster than a human second), so our efforts to keep up with the pace of life will only increase.

It needn't be this way. Throughout these years an ever increasing cadre of readers of *Becoming Stress-Resistant* has quietly benefited from the basic suggestions in this book. Although the nature of the age may change, the good news is that the basic biological and psychological components for good physical and mental health do not. This book with its scientifically-based research has distilled the basic skills necessary to reduce life stress, enhance productivity, improve the quality of life, and obtain peace of mind. While the reader will want to update the dollar cost figure on financial discussions in chapter seven to adjust for inflation, the basic principles in the book, including those for making important financial decisions, remain as accurate and as helpful as they have been for the past decade. These principles are readily learned.

Readers of *Becoming Stress-Resistant* have been able to cope successfully with the major life stresses noted above and will be better able to cope with those to come. You can join them and create less stressful, more meaningful lives for yourself and your loved ones. Since change is the only constant in nature, new stressful situations will emerge. Now is the time to become prepared, to become stress-resistant for the events that will unfold in the days to come.

—Raymond B. Flannery, Jr., PhD, FAPM
Autumn, 2003

PREFACE

Reasonable mastery of daily events, caring attachments to others, and a meaningful purpose in life are the three basic domains that lead to good physical and mental health and a sense of well-being (e.g., contentment, peace of mind, basic happiness, and satisfaction with one's self). Each of us needs these three general sets of abilities as we confront the stressful events of daily life that can befall any of us.

It is true that other books have been written about managing stress. I know. I have read most of them in my search for a good book on the topic to offer those I counsel, to my students, and to the staffs of corporations for whom I act as consultant. Many of these stress management books offer quick-fix answers, solutions of doubtful value in the short term and of even less help over the longer term. Others list several possible ways to cope, much like cookbook recipes, but the reader is left alone to sort out what would be useful for him or her. *None, however, has focused on the three essential domains of mastery, attachment, and meaning,* even though medicine and behavioral science have taught us that these are the keys to good health. This information is important to you and your loved ones, and to our nation as whole as we seek to contain ever-increasing medical costs. I have written this book to address this need, and it presents the comprehensive plan that shows you what to do so that you can feel well and enjoy your life.

For the past several years I have studied over 1,200 men and women to see who among them responded well to life stress and to learn what their adaptive strategies were. I have coined the term *Stress-Resistant Persons* to refer to these successful stress managers. Such persons utilize six specific characteristics to achieve reasonable mastery, to develop caring attachments to others, and to attain a meaningful purpose in life.

Reasonable mastery refers to the capacity or skills to shape and influence events in daily life so that their outcomes are beneficial to us. Stress-resistant persons use personal control, basic health practices, and a sense of humor to develop these reasonable mastery skills.

Caring attachments to others are the links or bonds that we have with other members of the human family. Stress-resistant persons know that such relationships to others provide psychological benefits such as better heart functioning. Stress-resistant persons use the skills of making a commitment to others, establishing a social network of friends, and being concerned for the welfare of others to establish caring attachments.

Stress-resistant persons also utilize concern for the welfare of others to attain a meaningful purpose in life. In this age of material acquisition, stress-resistant people seek to help others—not to attain the power, fame, and fortune that is often extolled as the central meaning in today's age. They know that being concerned for the welfare of others gives a meaningful purpose to life that material goods often do not, and that concern for the welfare of others helps us to cope more effectively with the stressful events in our own lives. This philosophic view of stress-resistant persons will help you keep life stress in perspective, and will enrich your understanding of when and why to choose the various coping strategies that we will discuss.

In the pages to follow, you will learn exactly what the six skills of stress-resistance are and how to incorporate them in your own life so that you will feel better as you confront the stresses of life. Many of my students and many of the people I have met in counseling have asked me to develop a program to help get them started on the road to better stress-resistance. Toward this end, I have developed a beginning program. It is called Project SMART (*Stress Management And Relaxation Training*), and it is presented here in detail so that you can implement it in your own life.

No matter what stress you face in life, you will find something of helpful interest in this book that will enhance your capacities for reasonable mastery, caring attachments, and purposeful meaning in life. My hope for each of you is that you enjoy these pages, and having read them, that your health and well-being improve.

An author's intellectual roots and indebtedness are many and diverse. Serious research such as reported in these pages requires earnest administrative support. I want to thank James A. Woods,

SJ, EdD, dean, and Rosemary Mohan, MEd, student services coordinator, of the Part-Time College at Boston College for their long and continuing support of the Stress-Resistance Project. I am equally appreciative of the support of Myron Belfer, MD, chair, Department of Psychiatry, the Cambridge (MA) Hospital, Harvard Medical School, and Mary Harvey, PhD, director of the hospital's Victims of Violence Program, in the implementation and assessment of Project SMART in the various programs of the hospital.

To the 1,200 men and women who have participated in my research, and to all the students and patients I have encountered over a twenty-year period, I thank you for what you have taught me about life and managing its stress.

Lastly, my gratitude to my family, my own teachers over the years, and to the following men and women who have directly assisted in the development of this book: William Bennett, MD; Matthew Bowen, PhD; Daniel Brown, PhD; Raymond Daly, PhD; Caroline Fish-Murray, EdD; Wallace Haley, MD; Judith Herman, MD; Thomas Garrett, PhD; Dennis Grossini; Henry Grunebaum, MD; Susan Johnson, EdD; Edward Khantzian, MD; William McArdle, MBA; John Mack, MD; Margaret May, Jr.; Kenneth Moritsugu, MD; Margaret Monahan; J. Christopher Perry, MD; Walter Penk, PhD; Mollie Schoenberg; Bessel van der Kolk, MD; Dow Weiman, Avery Weisman, MD; John Wissler, MBA, the late Norman Zinberg, MD; Robert Heller and Evander Lomke, my editors and friends at The Crossroad Publishing Company; and Norma Robbins, my helpful typist and caring critic, who on more than one occasion rose to the challenge of pulling it all together before yet another deadline. Their counsel has been wise and helpful. Any errors, however, remain my sole responsibility.

This book is about the importance of loving others. Toward that end, my wife Georgina has been research associate, reference librarian, teacher, caring spouse, and friend. Without her this book would not be.

—Raymond B. Flannery, Jr., PhD, FAPM
Autumn 1993

Author's Note and Editorial Method

This book is not intended to be a substitute for the medical advice of your physician or the counseling advice of your therapist. Everyone following the suggestions in this book is advised to begin with a physical exam to be sure that the symptoms you feel are stress-related and are not due to some other medical illness, and to have medical clearance for the aerobic exercise component of this book. Pay attention to the need for a balanced diet, and note carefully the specific warnings for the exercise and relaxation components of the program. Raise any questions that you may have with your physician, and always follow the advice of your physician first.

A Selected Reading list has been provided at the end of the volume for further reading as well as for all citations in the book.

* * *

All of the case examples in this book have been disguised to protect the anonymity of those involved.

Part 1

BECOMING STRESS-RESISTANT: A COMPREHENSIVE OVERVIEW

1

STRESS-RESISTANT PERSONS: REASONABLE MASTERY

Speak that I may know you.
—Ben Jonson

But I have promises to keep.
—Robert Frost

Blood surged in his temples. He could taste his anger. Neither he nor his eighteen-thousand-dollar vehicle were going anywhere fast. Bill Rockford had it all. Yet something was wrong, something was really wrong.

Late in the day on this final Tuesday of August, the temperature stood at ninety-seven degrees. He tapped impatiently on the steering wheel as he surveyed some of the meanest traffic the city could serve up. Damn the summer tourists. His body was stuck in the evening commute, his mind was stuck in a sandtrap.

His day had been another travesty. To start, he was more than forty minutes late. One car on the main artery had had one flat tire that caused citywide paralytic gridlock. He and Susan had had another argument before he had left for work, and now he learned that his business manager was out again, nursing an inflamed ulcer. Without breakfast and without the facts, he had had to wing it with the firm's most lucrative account. And so the day had gone. Half of a sandwich for a hasty lunch, two aspirins for his headache. And the phone calls. If he had had to return just one more call, he would have slammed the receiver into the wall. Now he sat, the blood surging in his veins.

He did seem to have it all. In his late forties, he was in the prime of his life. His company was successful. He had the "right" contacts, the "right" wife, and two children, one of whom could probably play football in a manner worthy of the Rockford family tradition.

He pushed yet another cigarette into his overweight body. A new home in an affluent suburb; a summer home on Cape Cod. If he had it all, why did it taste like ashes? Was all of life a traffic jam?

A screeching horn jarred him back to reality. He felt he could kill.

Does this sound familiar? You have your own set of circumstances, but I suspect the pileup of frustrations is painfully recognizable. Such is the stress of today's fast-paced life. The problems of Mr. Rockford's day captures the experience of many people's daily lives. In my counseling I hear these stress-related complaints in many different forms:

- A fifty-one-year-old male is referred with abdominal pain, a racing heart, and diarrhea. His company has just been purchased by a foreign bank, and his job is to be eliminated.

- A forty-two-year-old woman has recurring insomnia. Her husband, who began his social drinking in college, is now drinking daily because of the pressures at his small business, and is ruining the lives of his loved ones.

- A thirty-seven-year-old female comes for advice after three car accidents in two months. She is a manager in a computer firm, a single parent, and commutes two hours to work each way.

- A twenty-seven-year-old married male, complaining of ulcer pain, high blood pressure, and recurring head colds, has credit card debts in excess of eight-thousand dollars. His yearly income is twenty-nine-thousand dollars.

- A thirty-nine-year-old wife is suddenly experiencing tremors in her legs, and feelings of apprehension and panic. She thought she was happily married, but recently learned that her husband is having an affair with her best friend's daughter.

These individuals are not mentally ill; they are not going crazy as some of them fear; but they are, for the moment anyway, overwhelmed by the stress of life in the twentieth century. Their problems differ, but the sense of being unable to respond, to spring back quickly and get on with life, is common to all of them.

Nor are these men and women alone in feeling overburdened. A 1987 Harris poll found 89 percent of all Americans cited stress as a major problem in their lives. A great many of us feel unable to manage our daily lives, feel that we are caught on a treadmill, feel we are unable to slow down, to enjoy life.

This is a puzzling state of affairs for an affluent people. Up until 1900, keeping body and soul together was a daily hard-fought struggle. Just staying alive consumed all of one's energy and resources. Now we have time-saving devices like automobiles, jet aircraft, microwave ovens, and so forth to ease the burdens of life so it is bewildering that we still feel unable to catch up, let alone enjoy life.

Part of the explanation may lie in the fast pace of our culture. We are a mobile, restless people who pride ourselves on our cars and our freeway system, the symbols of our search for the good life. Yet the leading causes of car accidents are bald tires and empty gas tanks. One would think that such problems with something so important to us would and could be easily avoided, yet many of us seem to be unable to remember or too pressured for time to address even these most simple tasks. Our stress of life is often too intense for personal enjoyment. We feel overburdened. We feel cheated out of something that we can't really put our fingers on. We feel lonely at times, and very often we don't know what to do about it.

There are those among us, however, who seem better able to cope with the ups and downs of life, and to minimize the potential negative effects on health and well-being that such life stress can result in. I refer to these adaptive problem solvers as *Stress-Resistant Persons*. These are the men and women who carry on in the face of stress without becoming overwhelmed. Such men and women rarely feel cheated or lonely. To the contrary, they often retain a basic sense of contentment and perspective in the face of life's adversity. Clearly, they are "doing something right." This book looks in depth at how these stress-resistant persons cope, at how they utilize both reasonable mastery, and caring relationships or attachments to others, and at how they keep things centered so that they retain their health and well-being (Flannery, 1987a).

It is not that they *never* get demoralized, anxious or depressed, or physically ill. No human being is free from all life stress and all illness. Problems are a part of life, and the human person is built to respond to the challenge. Without problems we would wither. Stress-resistant people know this, but they are especially good at solving their problems with a *minimum* of disruption in their daily lives.

The good news is that we too can learn these adaptive skills. Our lives need not feel as unmanageable as Bill Rockford's seemed to be when we discussed his predicaments earlier in the chapter. Stress-resistant people can teach us how to manage stress so that we can be the best that we can be and enjoy life and the world about us.

To help us all get started toward developing these adaptive stress-resistant skills, I have devised the Project SMART program. It has helped many people learn the more adaptive coping strategies of stress-resistant persons. It can do the same for you, and I shall present the program in detail later in the book. But first we need to know more about stress-resistant people, and what is their special understanding of the importance of reasonable mastery and caring attachments. We begin with reasonable mastery.

Curiosity at Work

My own professional interest in such healthy people who coped adaptively began ten years ago. I was in charge of a psychiatric emergency room on one hot summer's day. The emergency room had been very busy that day, and the staff's nerves were frayed. Later in the evening, I was reflecting on how the heat was getting to people. I commented to the nurse how everyone had come to the emergency room that day. Then I realized I was wrong. Everyone had not come to the ER that day. In fact, some people never came at all. My professional curiosity was heightened. Were some people ashamed to come to a mental health service? Did they suffer in silence? Or were there persons who were truly able to cope with life's adversity? Were there helpful ways to manage life's inevitable traffic jams?

If such effective problem solvers existed, I had several questions to ask of them. What were their specific skills and general overall strategies for adapting to life stress? Were they born this way or did they learn their skills? If they learned them, who were their teachers? Was this capacity for coping well a function of one's sex or age, one's level of education, one's social class? Could the rest of us normal folks learn these better skills for coping? Could I find some way to teach these skills to my patients in order to minimize their future risk for illness?

While my questions were many, my answers were few. In a country that spent eleven percent of its gross national product on health care in 1988, there was remarkably little information and research on the personality characteristics of those who remained healthy in the face of life's problems.

My curiosity about the characteristics of people who remain healthy led me first to the writings of Plato and Aristotle. They observed the same phenomenon: some persons coped well with life's adverse circumstances, while others confronting apparently similar problems were overwhelmed and even crushed. They referred to the effective copers as well-ordered souls, and noted that such persons tended to take charge of their lives.

Hippocrates, the father of medicine and the first physician to catalogue most of our common medical problems, was also concerned with the person who was sick. He stated that he would rather know the person who had the disease than the disease that had the person. He too understood that the makeup of the person played an important role in the onset of illness as well as in the recovery process.

While medicine has a long and distinguished tradition of studying the relationship between life stress and subsequent illness, the relationship between life stress and subsequent health has received much less attention until very recently.

Lawrence Hinkle (Hinkle and Wolfe, 1958), a psychiatrist, is generally considered to have been the first person to systematically study healthy persons who coped well and avoided disease. In a series of studies over twenty years, Hinkle asked himself some very basic questions: Is illness a random event? Since germs surround us all the time, one would predict that one-seventh of the population would get sick on Sunday, one-seventh on Monday, and so forth till we were all sick. However, if the onset of illness was influenced by other factors in addition to the germs, then the illness onset would not be random. To assess this, he worked with the telephone company, and kept a simple count of the frequency of sick calls for each day of the week. What was his finding? He found that illness was not a random event. More people were sick on Mondays and Fridays than on other days of the week.

But why? Hinkle next gained permission from management and labor to contact employees in the telephone company who called in sick. They could volunteer to share what was happening in their lives when they became ill. Information was confidential and did not affect any evaluations of job performance. What did he find? The more life stress an employee had the greater the likelihood of getting sick. Although Hinkle did not realize it at the time, he was the first to document the process we have since clarified: under stress, our body's response to stress is activated, and our immune system, which protects us from some common types of illnesses, functions less efficiently. The person under stress is at risk for sickness.

Dr. Hinkle's research thus demonstrated that there are multiple risk factors for disease, not just the germ. For most scientists, these findings would be a source of great excitement in their own right, but not for Dr. Hinkle. His curiosity was aroused by yet another subgroup of telephone employees who had never called in sick. Was it that they had no life stress or were these employees well-ordered souls?

When he interviewed these people, it was clear to him that they were not free from life stress. Their lives were full of problems with money, work, and children, just like everyone else in the company. So how did they avoid illness? His findings provided the first clues that subsequent scientists and researchers have been building on.

The healthy employees coped in two clear ways. First, they took charge of their problems and their lives. They exercised mastery in resolving their own issues, and did not rely on others to do it for them. Secondly, these people had friends whom they could rely on, and they made new friends when they had to relocate. In taking charge of their personal lives, they reduced the intense arousal of the stress response; in being linked to others, they found comfort and support in life's darker moments. Reasonable mastery and caring attachments to others were the keys.

Others followed Hinkle's lead. The psychologist Robert White (1959) wrote a paper on competence. His paper has stood the test of time. White emphasized the importance of planned, orderly problem solving as a key in improving the quality of one's life. At the time he wrote this paper, planful, orderly people were considered old-fashioned and inhibited. But White was clear in his statements that "going with the flow" and living for the moment were detrimental to health.

Another psychologist, Abraham Maslow, built on this work, and in the 1960s studied self-actualizing people, persons who made the most of their talents and excelled in their chosen area of work. He proposed that human beings have a hierarchy of needs: physiological needs (sleep, food), safety needs (security, protection), social needs (acceptance, affection, love), esteem needs (power, status, achievement, autonomy), and finally, the need for self-actualization—the creative gift of using one's personal gifts to their fullest expression. Several research investigators have since demonstrated the importance of understanding these basic aspects of human development (Hennig and Jardin, 1977; Levinson, 1978; Vaillant, 1977). Meeting these human needs adequately avoids unnecessary life stress.

Still another important set of papers were written by psychologists, Doctors Salvatore Maddi and Suzanne Kobasa, in the 1970s. They studied business executives in an attempt to predict who would be healthy managers for their companies. Maddi and Kobasa identified three factors that predicted "hardy" personalities. They found that personal control, commitment to a task, and seeing problems as challenges rather than as burdens were associated with good health in these business persons (Maddi and Kobasa, 1984).

My own recent work extends these lines of inquiry. In addition to the basic problem of our limited knowledge in this area, the previous work raised three further issues for me. First, would the findings of Hinkle with working-class employees, and the findings of Maddi and Kobasa with upper-middle-class persons also be true for the large middle class? Were these ways of coping basic skills across peoples or were they a function of social class? Second, I wondered if the adaptive factors cited by Hinkle and Maddi and Kobasa were exhaustive of all the possible factors. Were these the only necessary skills or were there others of additional importance? Third, I wondered if these skills could be learned by less adaptive copers to enhance their ability to manage stress?

While my primary teaching responsibility is at Harvard Medical

School, for this type of research I needed healthy normal persons, not those who were already ill. For many years, I have been teaching in the Part-Time College at Boston College. The students in this program are adult men and women, many of whom work full-time, are heads of households, are enrolled full-time in the college's evening courses, and commute to campus in rush-hour traffic.

While many of the students come to class understandably tired at the end of a long day, there have always been a few who were full of energy and pep. At first I wondered if some might be using street drugs, but I soon realized that this was not true. Their high energy level was normal for them, and they were rarely sick and out of class. I was observing well-ordered souls. I wanted to understand what these men and women knew about dealing effectively with life stress, and set up my own long-term research project to answer this question.

Based on the previous research findings and my own clinical inferences, I began a series of studies to delineate their effective coping strategies. My research quickly established that there were three groupings of these adult students: some who were ill very frequently; some with average amounts of illness; and some who were rarely sick, the well-ordered souls. Using interviews, self-report measures, and behavioral observations, my associates and I have focused on the qualities of the third group of students, those students with the most effective ways of solving problems that lessen the negative impact on health. As I have noted earlier, I have coined the term *Stress-Resistant Persons* because the strategies for coping employed by these men and women resist or mitigate the potentially adverse impact of life stress on health and well-being.

My first research project goal was to provide additional research evidence about people who cope effectively and remain healthy. To date, the Stress-Resistance Project at Boston College has provided information on over 1,200 men and women from all walks of life. Each year we have studied a different group and they have ranged in age from seventeen to seventy-eight, and have a wide range of educational backgrounds.

These students have been primarily from the middle class. The results of these studies confirm the findings of Hinkle with working-class people, and of Maddi and Kobasa with upper-middle-class persons. There are, in fact, a basic set of skills for resisting the negative impact of life stress. Such skills are not dependent on one's social class or station in life, and there do not appear to be major gender differences. While there may be some constitutional factors that make it initially easier for some to learn some of these skills (Maddi and Kobasa, 1984), these are strategies for coping that can be mastered by everyone.

My second research goal was to ascertain if there were additional adaptive coping skills beyond those cited by previous investigators. The answer to this question is again yes. In a moment, I will summarize the findings of all of us who have studied people who problem-solve effectively so that you will better understand stress-resistant persons. You will note that most of the research agrees on the first four factors, that the Stress-Resistance Project has added two; and that several investigators, including my associates and myself, have completed some preliminary studies that are suggestive of additional factors that will need to be added to the list, if subsequent research confirms the early findings. Thus, the present list should not be considered exhaustive.

As of now, we do not know whether a stress-resistant person has to have all of these coping strategies or not. We also do not know whether some of these factors occur together naturally. These questions await further medical research. It does seem reasonable to assume that the more of these stress-resistant coping skills a person utilizes in the face of life stress, the greater will be the likelihood of solving the problem without disruptions to health and well-being.

Finally, my third research goal was to develop a way to teach these adaptive skills to those who did not know them. The goal was to reduce the potential negative impact on health and well-being from life stress as individuals acquired better skills for coping. As I have mentioned, the program that I have developed is called Project SMART. It is a program that will enable you to learn the skills of stress-resistant persons for yourself, and we shall study it in detail in chapter 6.

First, however, we need to understand fully the components that increase stress-resistance. Here is what we now know:

The Characteristics of Stress-Resistant Persons

What are the strategies that enable us to become more stress-resistant?

Personal Control. As can be seen in table 1, personal control is the first characteristic. It is a finding consistent in all of the research. You will have much better health if you personally attempt to exercise reasonable control of the stressful situation confronting you. The technical term for this process is *internal control.* It refers to the psychological state of self-initiated, self-directed problem solving. People who think of themselves as being in charge behave accordingly. Such persons size up the problem, and think out strategies to resolve it. Planned, organized self-directed behavior results in less stress and less subsequent illness. Such skills are the basis for reasonable mastery.

Many people rely on others to solve their problems for them. This psychological stance is known as *external control.* While all of us rely on others for help from time to time, externally controlled persons place the destiny of their lives completely in the hands of others. They give up direct control of the events in their lives. This is very simply a poor strategy. Only you know best what your needs are. No matter how well-intentioned the motives are of others coming to your aid, you know your needs most clearly. Continually relying on others to bail you out of life's problems results in more stress, more illness.

Task Involvement. Task involvement is the second characteristic of stress-resistant persons. All of us need a reason to live, a purpose in life. We need a task that we are personally or existentially committed to. For many of us this commitment could be to our families, careers, some community project, or hobby. It does not mean that we will always be happy and relaxed in pursuit of these goals, but it does mean that seeing these projects completed has some important personal meaning for us. Often these goals require the sacrifice of short-term pleasure. In the long haul, however, personal involvement in and commitment to a personally meaningful task leads to better individual health. Boredom, which is another way of describing lack of task involvement, is a powerful negative life stress in its own right and is better avoided. Stress-resistant people are rarely bored; they make it a point to find meaning in life.

Life-style Choices. There is a good deal of evidence that certain patterns of daily behavior employed by stress-resistant persons can be very helpful in reducing stress and its unwanted consequences.

Table 1

Stress-Resistant Persons:

1. Take Personal Control
2. Are Task Involved
3. Make Wise Life-Style Choices—Few Diet Stimulants
   —Aerobic Exercise
   —Relaxation Exercises
4. Seek Social Support
5. Have a Sense of Humor
6. Espouse Religious Values/Ethical Value of Concern for Others

These include a reduction in two dietary stimulants, and an increase in both aerobic exercise and relaxation exercises.

Dietary Stimulants. Caffeine and nicotine will cause the stress response in your body to increase *even when you have no problems.* As the stress response releases adrenalin, the person experiences anxiety. If the individual is anxious, he or she assumes there must be a problem. Since there is no obvious problem, the person creates one to explain the personal discomfort. Let me share with you a common example. Consider the following:

It is Monday morning after a "relaxing" weekend in which our vacationer wore himself out by trying to have it all. He leaves the house without breakfast and heads toward his entrance ramp on the expressway (a real misnomer, if ever there was one) for the commute to work. The radio reporter in the helicopter overhead announces there is a twelve-mile backup and everyone should come back on Wednesday. Our driver knows what to do. He pulls off the ramp, and heads for—where? The doughnut shop.

At the counter, our still sleepy driver orders coffee (caffeine). Not the standard cup, mind you, but the super giant fifteen-ounce one. Next come two of the finest chocolate-covered (caffeine) glazed cream-filled doughnuts that the store ever made. As our hero consumes these foods, his stress response goes into overdrive with a ferocity that would scare a gorilla. Our driver with his increasing sense of excitation incorrectly labels his internal medical crisis as "waking-up." To celebrate his finally seeing the dawn's early light, he lights up a cigarette (nicotine), and then heads downtown in the morning traffic.

Forty minutes later, he parks his car, and emerges shaking like a leaf. He then compounds his problems by again incorrectly labeling his current state of affairs. He cites the traffic as the source of his distress and misses the impact of his breakfast altogether. Stress-resistant people know better than this. They know they should minimize their use of caffeine and nicotine as a general strategy for managing stress.

Aerobic Exercise. Aerobic or hard exercise is the second life-style strategy employed by successful copers. Aerobic exercise is exercise that stimulates the functioning of the heart muscle. Like any muscle in the body, the heart needs to be toned to ensure its correct functioning.

Common forms of aerobic exercise include swimming or jogging. An adequate exercise program can take as little as three twenty-minute periods stretched over a week. Hard exercise tones the heart muscle, tones down the stress response, increases perceptual clarity, and induces a sense of well-being. Adequate copers do not forego this set of bonuses.

Relaxation Exercises. I have never met a stress-resistant person who did not have time to relax. They understand the benefits for stress management, and they put aside at least fifteen minutes each day for deep breathing, meditation, prayer, and the like. Stress-resistant people often use a fifteen-minute relaxation period just before some predictable life stress, such as exam taking or public speaking.

Social Support. Social support or caring attachments is another characteristic of stress resistance. It refers to the helpful interactions we have with other human beings. In these caring relationships we form bonds with others and become attached to them. The physical and psychological benefits of these attachments is so important and so complex that they will be spelled out in detail in the next chapter.

To these four common characteristics of stress-resistant persons, my colleagues and I would add two additional components that we have identified:

Humor. Humor helps to reduce stress because it helps us to see the paradoxes in life that befall all of us. It helps us keep problems in perspective, and appears to reduce the physiology of stress.

Stress-resistant persons use their sense of humor, or associate with those who have one.

Religious Values. The great religions of the world have always stressed concern for the welfare of others: love one another. We wondered if such a value code made any sense in an industrial/corporate age of individual competitiveness, and conducted research to investigate this issue. Stress-resistant people have known the answer all along. While they work to attain the gains of technology, they have not lost sight of the importance of caring for others, of helping others, of following the Golden Rule. They may not be active church, synagogue, or mosque attendees, but the decisions that guide their daily lives are influenced by ethical regard for others. Like the previous five characteristics, adhering to the basic principle of concern for others results in less stress and improved health.

Let me state again that this list is not yet complete. Some early studies suggest that a sense of optimism, and a sense of coherence or framework for integrating life's events may well need to be added to our list. We are in the early stages of understanding the personalities of such stress-resistant persons. Undoubtedly, we will learn more.

In the meantime, do these factors have anything else in common? Do they have anything else to tell us? I think so.

As we have noted, reasonable mastery and caring attachments are the basic markers for good physical and mental health. If we reflect on the six characteristics of stress-resistant persons, we find both reasonable mastery and caring attachments. Personal control, lifestyle choices, and a sense of humor are all strategies for attaining reasonable mastery. Just as these tie together, so do task involvement, social support, and religious values. These latter three form the basis for caring attachments and relatedness to others. These three also form the basis for developing the values and attitudes of caring for and sharing with others.

From these six characteristics emerges the philosophy of stress-resistance that we have noted: reasonable mastery; the basic stress management practices of balanced diet, aerobic exercise, and relaxation periods; caring attachments to others, and a concern for helping others, for loving others.

Such stress-resistant people have much to teach us and we shall explore their helpful ways in the pages to follow.

Reasonable Mastery: Some Basics

Having reviewed the general characteristics of stress-resistant persons, let us first turn our attention to some specific components of control, which, if successfully mastered, can enhance our capacity to buffer life stress.

Robert Allen (1981) has developed an interesting chart to help any of us gauge our life expectancy. I have included it in table 2. The questions, particularly in the life-style section, will provide some initial guidance as to the areas in which we may need to exercise reasonable mastery. Pay particular attention to the questions that result in the subtraction of points.

Table 2

Life-Expectancy Chart:
___

While there is no sure way to calculate your life expectancy even with computer systems, there are certain guidelines, such as this test, that can give you rough estimates. If you are age twenty to sixty-five and reasonably healthy, this test provides a life insurance company's statistical view of your life expectancy.

Start with the number 72

Personal Data:
   If you are male, **subtract three.**
   If female, **add four.**
   If you live in an urban area with a population over two million,
      subtract two.
   If you live in a town under 10,000 or on a farm, **add two.**
   If a grandparent lived to eighty-five, **add two.**
   If all four grandparents lived to eighty, **add six.**
   If either parent died of a stroke or heart attack before the age of fifty,
      subtract four.
   If any parent, brother, or sister under fifty has (or had) cancer or a
      heart condition, or has had diabetes since childhood, **subtract
      three.**
   Do you earn over $50,000 a year? **Subtract two.**
   If you finished college, **add one.** If you have a graduate or professional
      degree, **add two more.**
   If you are sixty-five or over and still working, **add three.**
   If you live with a spouse or friend, **add five.** If not, **subtract one** for
      every ten years alone since age twenty-five.

Healthstyle facts:

If you work behind a desk, **subtract three.**

If your work requires regular, heavy physical labor, **add three.**

If you exercise strenuously (tennis, running, swimming, etc.) five times a week for at least a half-hour, **add four.** Two or three times a week, **add two.**

Do you sleep more than ten hours each night? **Subtract four.**

Are you intense, aggressive, easily angered? **Subtract three.**

Are you easygoing and relaxed? **Add three.**

Are you happy? **Add one.** Unhappy? **Subtract one.**

Have you had a speeding ticket in the last year? **Subtract one.**

Do you smoke more than two packs a day? **Subtract eight.** One to two packs? **Subtract six.** One-half to one? **Subtract three.**

Do you drink the equivalent of a quart bottle of liquor a day? **Subtract one.**

Are you overweight by fifty pounds or more? **Subtract eight.** By thirty to fifty pounds? **Subtract four.** By ten to thirty pounds? **Subtract two.**

If you are a man over forty and have annual checkups, **add two.**

If you are a woman and see a gynecologist once a year, **add two.**

Age adjustment:

If you are between thirty and forty, **add two.**

If you are between forty and fifty, **add three.**

If you are between fifty and seventy, **add four.**

If you are over seventy, **add five.**

Add up your score to get your life expectancy at this time. Now compare it to the national averages, which are about seventy-five years for males, and seventy-eight years for females.

> From *Lifegain* by Robert F. Allen, Ph.D., with Shirley Linde, New York: Appleton Century Crofts, 1981, pp. 19–20.

*   *   *

With your life-expectancy score as a guide, let us examine some of the basic strategies for establishing reasonable mastery.

Biological Limitations. Each of us needs to be aware of any acute/chronic illness that will impair the physiology of the body to respond in its fullest capacity. Arthritis, diabetes, and vision problems are examples of limitations that require extra adjustments when dealing with life stress. We need to make allowances for them.

Optimal Level of Stimulation. Your nervous system and mine is built to take in information about the world around us through our senses: hearing, taste, touch, smell, vision. How much information we are able to absorb without being psychologically taxed is in part a biological process that we are born with. It is referred to as an optimal level of stimulation: that point at which we take in enough information so that we are neither bored (too little) nor overwhelmed (too much).

People seem to be born with predominantly one of these two types of optimal levels of stimulation. Persons who biologically need lesser amounts to feel comfortable and efficient are referred to as introverts. Such persons are generally quiet, reflective, interested in nature, ethics, study. They like quiet times and a few close friends.

Persons who need a good deal of stimulation to feel comfortable are called extroverts. Persons in this second group like great amounts of activity, large parties, a great array of hobbies, friends, and so forth.

While all of us have quiet moments as well as periods of busy activity, our nervous systems seem predominantly wired to be one type or the other. One helpful way to determine your basic type is to keep a daily log of the frequencies and types of your daily activities for two weeks. Stress-resistant people realize that it's important to know which group you belong to. One can then gear the pace of one's life to what feels comfortable biologically.

Problem Solving. One of my patients once told me that half his problem was in his head and the rest of it was in his mind. An overstatement to be sure, but like all such statements it contains some truth. The capacity to think and reason clearly is an important component in coping with stress.

It is amazing to see the number of people running about solving the wrong problem. Time and time again, I have observed people confronted with life stress get anxious, angry, or depressed, and rush off to solve the problem before they take the time to understand the real issue and what is the most reasonable way to approach it. In a small book like this, there is no way to teach the complex skills of problem solving, but there are some very useful general guidelines that skilled problem-solvers use.

1. Identify the real issue. We humans have a remarkable capacity to lose our focus when we are distressed, so the first step is to clarify the specific problem before us. What exactly is the life stress? What has been our response in terms of feelings? When did these feelings start? Whom was I with? What was I doing? What was I thinking? These types of questions help to clarify the true nature of the event. For example, Ellen woke up depressed this morning. Is it because it is a rainy day or is she sad because it is the anniversary of her friend's death? A parent is angry with the child. Did the child really do anything to get the parent this angry, or has the child become the focus of anger the adult feels toward someone else like a spouse, or boss?

2. Gather information to solve the problem. History repeats itself so whatever problems we face, we can be reasonably confident that someone else has confronted this problem before us. Ask other people what they have done in similar situations. Read books and articles. Use your library. Libraries contain many of the solutions

Reasonable Mastery Requires That We Be Prepared.

"I found the bullets!"

to life's problems that have been tried by persons who have lived before us. We live in a complex technological age, and we will cope more effectively the greater the amount of information we have at hand.

3. Develop plans to solve the problem. Because of the intricacy of most problems, our capacity to cope is enhanced by developing several strategies to solve any problem, and implementing one or more potential solutions as needed. It is better not to have all of your eggs in one basket. Have several courses of action, and prioritize them. Do not assume that your first strategy will work. If you are interviewing for a new job, for example, rehearse various answers to any of the more standard questions an interviewer will probably ask.

4. Implement a strategy and evaluate it. Put your course of action into motion, and then evaluate it to see whether it in fact solved the problem. We are all too busy doing too many things, and we find it easier to assume that everything is back on track and moving smoothly. Yet human experience often challenges this assumption. Relationships come apart, expected promotions don't happen, families end up in misunderstandings. Persistence leads to effective problem solving. Be sure to leave time to evaluate your solution, and time to try another strategy if the first one appears to fail. Our society is too complex for everything to run smoothly. Communications problems are common in our society. If you have had a disagreement with someone that you feel you both have discussed and resolved, check a day or two later to be sure the new resolution is clear to both of you.

Reasonable Expectations. In my twenty years of counseling, I have observed many people fail at solving problems they could solve because their expectation of what the outcome should be was incorrect. I have seen very bright people aim too low in their expectations, and remain depressed and unmotivated. I have seen others set superhuman goals, goals beyond the capacity of anyone to attain. In aiming too high, they succeeded only in making themselves extremely anxious. A person with an intelligence level of over 140 is very bright. In choosing a career waiting on tables, the person's low expectations will lead to depression. A person of average intelligence who insists on being a president of a Fortune 500 company without having had any schooling has created a task that no human person could reasonably expect to succeed at.

Stress-resistant persons intuitively understand the importance of having reasonable expectations about themselves and others. They head for the middle ground between too low and too high while they retain a sense of humor and optimism. They know that mastery has its limits. There are many problems that we have in life that we cannot solve such as the death of a loved one, the abuse of drugs by an adult we love, and so forth. Stress-resistant people know this well, and thus set reasonable mastery as their goal, not complete mastery. Their religious values can be helpful to them here. Religion not only steers us toward concern for others, it also helps us to explain and live with our to-be-expected human failures. After repeated attempts to solve the problem as best they can, stress-resistant people can deal with a negative outcome. "It was God's will" or "It is in the hands of God now" are statements that keep life stress in perspective, and allow the individual to let go of solving the problem. The stress is reduced, and the person moves on in life.

An awareness of our biological limitations, our basic type of optimal level of stimulation, the fundamental components of problem solving, and a set of reasonable expectations of ourselves and others are helpful basic steps in moving towards the goal of reasonable mastery.

Some Thoughts as We Begin

Our physical brain contains a structure called the *locus coeruleus*. Its function is to produce some of the chemicals that you and I ultimately experience as stress-related anxiety. Some researchers believe that between the ages of forty to sixty the *locus coeruleus* gradually releases these chemicals less frequently. Thus, one way to cope with stress is to wait until you become middle-aged. That can be a long time to wait if you are young and anxious, and you can still have many stress-related problems in middle age and beyond. It really is not a good coping strategy.

It is better to work toward developing the various characteristics of stress-resistant persons gradually over time. We have focused on reasonable mastery in this chapter, and we shall explore caring attachments in the next. There is no quick fix to becoming stress-resistant. Human growth is most effectively dealt with in small, manageable steps. Coping with stress is no exception to this rule.

As we implement the various aspects of managing stress, we shall feel better. However, we need to have reasonable expectations about stress resistance as a goal. It may take us two years or longer to implement the major lifestyle shifts outlined in this book in such manageable steps. Self-reflection, self-assessment, and discussing these issues with others can also help us as we go along.

2

STRESS-RESISTANT PERSONS: CARING HUMAN ATTACHMENTS

The eyes are blind, one must look with the heart.
—Saint Exupéry

Complete possession is proved only by giving.
—André Gide

White and red light reflected off of her face in the darkness as if she were dancing at some late-night disco. She was on a high, and it had nothing to do with drugs, sex, alcohol, power, or money. Her high was life itself.

Maybe her friends were right when they noticed her zest for life. Maybe she was more buoyant than they were; she certainly didn't seem to be sick as often as they were. Maybe she was born this way. She had never really given it much thought.

Donna was a remarkable person, even her ex-husband admitted that, and he rarely had anything nice to say about anyone. Here she was: an assistant manager at the bank, a single parent of a teenager, the primary caretaker of her invalid mother, and a full-time student in the evening college where she was completing her bachelor's degree.

Donna moved from task to task with grace. While most of her friends would have been overwhelmed by her range of commitments, Donna went about her routine with order, ease, a sense of humor, and an occasional silent prayer. She certainly didn't feel overburdened. Life was an interesting challenge for her to be pursued in full and reasoned measure each day. With regular exercise, a sensible diet, and some time to rest each day, Donna found that she was rarely overtired or unable to respond. Her life was full, her friends were dear, she did what she could to help others.

Even now as she sat in some of the meanest rush hour traffic in the city on her way to class, she reflected on the beauty of the falling snow. Headlight white and taillight red made an interesting collage of this evening snowfall. She was grateful for the snow and for her day. Others blew their horns in anger, and hurled expletives towards other iced-over windows. Donna sat there quietly, and enjoyed the peace of the snowfall. She had promises to keep.

Unlike Bill Rockford in chapter 1, Donna exemplifies the characteristics of a stress-resistant person. She dealt with her day's events and traffic jams in ways quite different from Mr. Rockford. She utilized the reasonable mastery skills that we outlined in the last chapter, and she remained close to her caring attachments.

The need for another human being is deeply rooted in each of us. All of us want to be loved; and all of us have at some time felt alone and abandoned. We have needed others. Where have you experienced this universal human longing? Were you home alone sick for an extended period of time? Did your spouse suddenly walk out of your life? Did you bury a loved one? Were you isolated in your laboratory or at your word processor? Were you an older person who saw your family too infrequently? Were you mentally ill, physically handicapped, homeless, or shunned by most of the rest of society because of your color or your race? You and I have all experienced this aloneness, this need to be with another human being, this desire to be accepted even with our human failings and limitations.

My own interest in these matters was sharpened by a question from one of my evening college students. Stress-resistant people value highly the attachments they have to others and leave time to develop such relationships, and I was communicating to the class this stress-resistant wisdom of caring for others. A hand went up, and a student asked me why he should do this, what was in it for him. I reiterated the collective wisdom of stress-resistant people. He was unmoved. I reminded him that God told us to love one another. He snickered, and I thought about the narcissism that echoed in the silence of my classroom. His question led me to spend the next three years reviewing all the research on human attachment and social support to see what the medical and scientific research had revealed, the findings that stress-resistant people knew about intuitively.

The truth of such matters is remarkable. There appears to be a very powerful set of links between the biology of the body and the presence of others. So great is this interaction that we communicate it in our language: "Let me call you sweetheart . . . ," "You touch me . . . ," "Absence makes the heart grow fonder . . . ," "She died of a broken heart . . . ." Dr. James Lynch (1977) has given us one very dramatic example of the power of human contact. A middle-aged man was brought by the police to a medical service in a deep coma. His vital signs were ebbing, he was dying. No one knew him, and he had no known relatives to contact. As he slipped towards the silence of death, one of the nurses held his hand in compassion. His vital signs (blood pressure, heart rate) all strengthened. Here was powerful health-giving contact between two human beings, yet both were complete strangers and one was in a coma.

The presence of others is a very powerful force in dealing with life's problems. Other persons help us to work toward solving our problems, but they also literally improve our physical health and our psychological sense of well-being. Our presence also provides these benefits to others.

As we begin our review of what is known, a few questions may help to focus our understanding of these findings. Why do stress-resistant people value such attachments? In what ways do other members of the human family enhance our physical vitality? What are the specific psychological exchanges that occur that lead to a sense of well-being? Where are such helpful relationships to be found? Can relationships be harmful? How could one tell the difference? When you meet someone for the first time, is there any way to know whether the relationships will be for good or ill?

The Nature of Human Attachments

Human attachment may be defined as the comfort, assistance, and/or information one receives through formal (class, work, church) or informal (parties, casual gatherings) contacts with individuals and groups. These helpful contacts may be verbal, such as when people tell us they care about us or give us advice, or they may be nonverbal, such as when someone gives us a hug or helps us to cross the street. While human attachment and social support have differing specific meanings in scientific research, for our purposes here there is enough overlapping meaning to use this definition as our general guideline.

Our need for attachment appears to be biologically rooted (Bowlby, 1969), and present at birth. These human links appear indispensable for physical safety, for emotional comfort, and for both short- and long-term survival of each of us.

At the turn of our century, the well-known sociologist, Emile Durkheim, predicted that human beings would be disrupted from their care-taking groups as we moved toward our industrial/corporate age. He feared that the loss of such attachments would adversely affect the health and well-being of society. A wealth of medical evidence supports his view. As people have moved towards material acquisition and away from lesser involvement with others, the absence of these attachments has led to sharp increases in demoralization, anxiety, and depression, the onset of physical illnesses and psychosomatic disease, and even premature death. You and I could die from a broken heart. Stress-resistant people are correct in insisting on the importance of caring attachments as a resource for responding to life stress.

How do we form such caring human attachments? There have been two main explanations.

Dr. John Bowlby, the British psychoanalyst (1969), focuses on the role of the mother in parenting. He believes that children are born with the need for social interaction as we have noted. He feels that physical contact with adults—particularly with the mother—is the way this need first expresses itself. If adults and mothers provide consistent, caring, and adaptive mothering in response to the infant's calls for closeness, a sound basis for secure infant attachments occurs. Such secure infant attachment is thought to lead to subsequent adaptive adult development.

The second explanation has been provided by Dr. Henry Goldsmith (Flannery, 1990). Dr. Goldsmith emphasizes the importance of the infant's temperament. Infants temperamentally prone to distress through fear or anger are usually harder to care for. They develop less satisfactory social interchanges with adults and mothers because they resist such potentially beneficial contacts and frustrate the care givers. These disruptions of the parent-child bonding process lead to insecurity with others later on.

There is some research evidence to support both views (Flannery,

1990). Much further inquiry, however, is needed before we can be fully assured of each theory. It may well be proven that the infant's temperament and the mother's parenting skills are both important, and it really is not known as yet whether these explanations will adequately explain the full range of adult relationships. This research, however, does provide some helpful suggestions as to how this process may begin.

Caring Attachments and Human Physiology

Medicine has long understood the curative power that a doctor has when he or she places his or her hand on an ill patient. Likewise, the will to live itself appears to be strengthened by human interaction and concern for others. We all know of examples where someone was terminally ill, but lived long enough to see his or her child graduate or get married. Since the majority of tasks that you and I must cope with in life involve interaction with others, it should not surprise us that the presence of others can influence the physiological processes in both parties. Nor should it surprise us when we learn that the presence of others can be helpful or harmful to our health, depending on the nature of the interaction. What has not been clear is how this happened.

Now, however, medical and scientific research have given us some beginning explanations of these events. It is true that these are very complicated and interwoven biological processes. It is also true that medicine is only at the beginning of its studies, yet there now is enough evidence to suggest how the presence of others may affect our heart (the cardiac system), our ability to fight disease (the immune system), and probably our sense of well-being (the endogenous opioid system). Nature is sharing some of her secrets with us.

The Cardiac System. Physicians through the centuries have continuously recorded that certain patients have died suddenly when strong passions had been stirred in them by others (Engel, 1971). Sudden heart disease was a frequent finding in these deaths. With heart disease our nation's number one health problem, anything we can do to further our understanding of the cause of this disease will be helpful.

Medical research has already identified certain risk factors that make any of us more prone to heart disease. These include high blood pressure, high levels of serum cholesterol, cigarette smoking, and the like. However, as the research evidence accumulates, it is becoming clear that the absence of caring human attachments may be another risk factor to be added to the list.

Numerous studies conducted in various countries over many years indicate that social isolation, sudden loss of loved ones, and chronic human loneliness may seriously contribute to disruptions in normal cardiac functioning, and cause serious heart disease and even premature cardiac-related death (House, Landis, Umberson, 1988). The presence of caring others is directly linked to health and well-being.

Dr. James Lynch and his colleagues (1977, 1985) have begun through extensive research efforts to identify how the presence of caring others may lead to these documented cardiovascular benefits. The presence of caring others may stabilize and strengthen heart rate, and stabilize and lower blood pressure. Conversely, harmful human attachments appear to lead to dysfunction in these same processes. If we think back to the man in the coma whose vital signs were strengthened by a nurse he did not know, we have a clear example of the power of caring others to enhance these basic heart functions.

Of the many types of relationships that people may form, marriage appears to be one of the more potentially powerful for regulating cardiac functioning over time. Back in 1957, two researchers, Drs. Arthur Kraus and Abraham Lilienfeld, demonstrated that the unmarried had increased rates of death when compared with their married counterparts. This finding has been demonstrated repeatedly in subsequent research. For both sexes, for all ages, and for all races, the unmarried have a higher rate of premature death from heart disease (Lynch, 1977). This is true even if you are young. Married women between the ages of twenty-five and thirty who are widowed have at least a two times greater chance of heart disease than married women of the same age. Marriage is an important consideration for health and longevity. (There is no information available as yet about healthy hearts and living together.)

Disruption in human attachments is similarly linked to increased susceptibility to heart disease and premature death from heart disease. Such findings have been reported for persons who lost a parent early in life, for persons grieving the loss of a loved one, and for persons for whom dying will resolve a long-standing interpersonal conflict (Lynch, 1977). For example, Dr. George Engle (1971) in a study of recently deceased people found that the person's sudden and unexpected death was frequently preceded by the immediate severing of a bond with a loved one through death, job relocation, or a bitter estrangement. Drs. Weisman and Hackett (1961) in another example of such findings reported on seven people undergoing minor surgery. All of them died on the operating table, and none appeared to die from surgical complications. A review of their surgical cases indicated that these patients were prepared to die: some to join a deceased loved one, others because they had no one on earth to live for.

Not everyone who has lost attachments dies prematurely. Such losses and their impact are complicated life events. Undoubtedly, we will learn more about these processes as research continues, but these findings already demonstrate the important, healing relationships between caring attachments and cardiac functioning. Without such attachments, it seems that people can die from a broken heart.

The Immune System. The immune system is that part of our bodies that fights disease. It does this by attacking the germs directly and in part by repairing the wear and tear on our bodies. It is a very complex system with many component parts. Different parts of the immune system respond in a variety of ways to the many different types of life stress. When confronted with these various life problems, the immune system functions less efficiently and leaves the individual at increased risk of susceptibility to some common diseases, including infectious diseases and allergies as well as to more serious disorders such as AIDS, or rheumatoid arthritis.

The presence of caring others appears to enhance the capacity of the immune system to resist our getting sick. Likewise, the disruption of such attachments may result in illness. Bereavement, poor marriages, separations, divorce, and chronic human loneliness have all been associated with poor immune functioning (Kiecott-Glasser & Glasser, 1986). Bereaved and divorced persons in particular have been shown to have higher rates of disease and premature death. Caring attachments seem to be a resource for maintaining good health in the presence of life stress.

The Endogenous Opioid System. One of the more exciting recent discoveries in medicine has been the discovery in the brain of chemicals called endorphins and enkephalins. These substances circulate in the brain and appear to minimize feelings of pain and depression. Endorphins are similar in chemical structure to opiates; and like opiates, which are known for their pain-killing properties, endorphins appear to act as analgesics.

Endorphins not only diminish feelings of pain, but they also appear to contribute to making us feel good, upbeat, less anxious, and content. "Runner's high" medically refers in part to the increased endorphin stimulation produced by aerobic exercise.

Under stress endorphins function less efficiently just as the immune system does. Since the research in this area has only just begun, we must exercise caution in drawing inferences from these studies. However, the early studies do in fact suggest that life stress diminishes endorphin response (Beutler et al, 1986). Since much of life stress involves human interaction, it seems reasonable to assume that in time the absence of attachments will be shown to affect opioid response negatively.

Future research will no doubt clarify the role of attachments and human physiological functioning. Other aspects of human biological functioning may be added to the list. In any case, the evidence to date provides important indications of how the presence of caring others can be a resource for stress resistance in coping with life stress.

Caring Attachments and Human Psychology

The reports of improved physical and mental health in caring relationships has led to a search for those encounters that are helpful, those that are harmful, and where such interchanges may take place.

Helpful Exchanges. Investigators have found at least four types of interchanges that are helpful, lead to stress resistance, and result in improved health and well-being. These are presented in table 1. This list should not be considered exhaustive. It reflects what helpful exchanges medical science knows about presently.

Emotional Support. When we are unhappy, lonely, angry, or excited and joyful, we want to share these feelings with others, to let them know about us and our lives. This is the first beneficial way helpful interchanges can occur. Emotional support helps us to

Table 1

The Psychology of Human Attachment

Factors in Helpful and Harmful Human Attachments	
HELPFUL	*HARMFUL*
Emotional Support	Value Conflicts
Information	Emotional Demandingness
Social Companionship	Emotional Overinvolvement
Instrumental Support	Interpersonal Skill Deficiency

share our burdens, minimizes our sense of being alone, and gives us the courage to go on. Such exchanges are important for our self-esteem even if there is nothing we can do about the problem (e.g., the death of a loved one).

Information. Information is a helpful interchange because it can reduce life stress by spelling out possible strategies to solve any given problem, by suggestions about how long it might take to resolve the problem, or even by pointing out that the problem is insoluble and that the person is doing as well as can reasonably be expected. Information exchanges are good examples of how caring relationships can increase reasonable mastery.

Social Companionship. In my years of counseling I have often heard people of all ages express the common human feeling of loneliness, and of the desire to be with someone to escape its burden. Children, single adults, and our elderly often feel this way. The presence of others reduces our sense of helplessness, vulnerability, and aloneness. Sharing the human journey with another provides meaning to the events of daily life.

Instrumental Support. When others offer us tangible help in dealing with life stress, they are providing us with instrumental support. Most common among these are offers of money, material goods, and political favors. These materials enhance the individual's capacity to respond to the problem before him or her. Giving gifts is a common way in our culture to offer caring instrumental response.

Of four factors that we know about at this time, emotional

support and information seem to be general strategies for solving a range of problems. Social companionship and instrumental support seem more helpful in specific situations. These four helpful strategies also enhance our sense of reasonable mastery, and thus additionally increase our ability to resist the potential negative effects of stress. Stress-resistant persons utilize these helpful exchanges in their efforts for others.

Harmful Exchanges. As we all know from personal experience, not all interchanges are helpful and pleasant. Some make us feel worse. Some are even destructive. Consider the following.

Tomorrow would be three years to the day. She sat alone at the back of the airport chapel. Numb now to the grief and the sorrow, she sat in near desolation. Cut off from everyone. Alone. Lonely. She wondered if you really could die from a broken heart.

That special morning had dawned full of sunshine and hope. She and her George would spend that spring Saturday at a beach picnic. She began her day with a brief prayer as was her custom: thanking God for her family and friends, her job, but mostly for George. They had been engaged for three months now, and Helen felt proud and honored to be his chosen one. She would work so hard for better or for worse. Her heart was filled with anticipatory excitement. She loved him so.

With breakfast done, she had gone to the market for chips and soda for their picnic celebration. As she unlocked the door to her apartment, one hand grabbed her wrist, the other covered her mouth. The burglar disrobed her as she fought with all her strength; he forced himself upon her virgin self with an ugliness beyond words. She felt dirty as if she were a woman of the streets. Her heart sank into utter despair.

George held her tightly. Her parents and brother and friends had been initially outraged; but as the defense attorney continuously portrayed her as inciting the rape, one by one they fell away. Even her own family blamed her in the end, but it was the note of leave taking from George that crushed her heart.

The assailant was ultimately sentenced to three years in jail for armed robbery. Tomorrow he would be free. Perhaps they were right, perhaps she had done something wrong. She sat alone in the darkness of the chapel in one of the busiest airports in the United States. Helen wondered if God was with her; she wondered if anyone cared.

*   *   *

As Helen's pain makes clear, not all relationships and human interchanges are helpful, and table 1 also lists the four types of harmful interchanges. The research evidence here is more limited at the moment, so that the list of harmful exchanges should be viewed as guidelines to what may cause problems between people.

Helpful attachments can be lost through common events such as death, job relocation, the children leaving home. Helpful attachments can also be lost because the other may feel overwhelmed by our problems or their own. They can further be disrupted if the parties have differing goals, or say something in anger that hurts the other's feelings. In these examples, even though the outcome was harmful, both parties were well intentioned, and life events or life stress disrupted the relationship. Table 1, however, lists the types of harmful interchanges which are consistent patterns of responding and which are often done with ill will. They are fundamentally poor strategies for coping, and they lower stress resistance.

Value Conflicts. None of us can agree on everything. There is a plurality of choices and events, and life would be dull if we all viewed the world the same way. However, relationships marked by fundamental and far-reaching differences of opinion increase life stress. If you are a peace advocate, and your spouse makes napalm, you have a fundamental, far-reaching conflict. If you feel children should be raised strictly, and your mate believes in free and unfettered expression, you have a fundamental difference. Attitudes toward career aspiration, money and credit, material goods, the basic meaning of life are common examples of areas of potential disagreement. The greater the number of fundamental value conflicts, the greater is the potential for disruption in the relationship.

Emotional Demandingness. When one party in a relationship is always demanding that things be done in one way, or is always monopolizing the time in the relationship, or must always be the center of attention, that person has created a state of emotional demandingness. This taxing of the provider's goodwill and resources will eventually result in emotional exhaustion, anger, and avoidance on the part of the provider.

Emotional Overinvolvement. Overinvolvement is a similar process of overtaxing the relationship. In this case, one party is attempting to use excessive control over the other in unhealthy ways.

Excessive overprotection, intrusiveness, and excessive self-sacrifice are frequently associated with negative feelings and the end of the relationships.

Interpersonal Skill Deficiency. Relationships characterized by conflict induced because one or both members are deficient in interpersonal skills is the fourth type of harmful interchange. Most of us continue to grow and mature in our capacity to interact with others, but sometimes this does not happen either because there was no one to learn from or the role models themselves used harmful exchanges. For example, in marriage the partners may not know how to budget time or money; in raising children the parents may not know how to impose discipline or provide comfort; at work the employee may strive only for him or herself rather than the whole work unit. Such skill deficiency can be found in marriages, child-rearing, and at work. These deficiencies usually leave all parties feeling miserable. If the skill deficiency is in the marriage relationship, other caring attachments do not appear to mitigate its harmful consequences. Lastly, relationships marked by physical, sexual, extreme verbal abuse and/or neglect are relationships in which all four of these harmful exchanges are often present. Physical safety and basic prudence necessitate change in such relationships.

Where These Interactions Occur: Networks and Buffers. Both helpful and harmful exchanges can occur in two formats that have been delineated by research thus far.

Networks are the first way, and refer to those social structures of daily life in which a person is embedded. These might include one's biological family, extended family, marriage and children, work relationships, and church and community links. Networks are thought to provide each of us with a sense of stability, access to general problem-solving information, and increased self-esteem from group acceptance.

Buffers are the second structure for interpersonal exchange. Buffers are persons who provide us with special knowledge to solve specific problems when we are faced with intense life stress. The buffer may or may not be in one's networks. Physicians, lawyers, and the clergy could be examples of buffers that might not be in one's networks. The beneficial buffering or mitigating effects of such buffering attachments are thought to stem from their ability to augment our sense of reasonable mastery and to help us avoid a feeling of helplessness when faced with very serious stressful situations.

All of us can potentially benefit from the helpful resources available in both networks and buffers as we progress through our lives. The better the networks and buffers, the greater the number of helpful exchanges, the greater will be our capacity for stress resistance in dealing with life stress. The power of caring attachments that stress-resistant persons utilize so well is available to each of us.

Caring Human Attachments: Some Basics

Let us now turn to some of the basic issues for people to discuss to ensure helpful relationships: starting, sustaining, and ending relationships in ways that enhance stress resistance.

Starting Relationships. In my counseling experience the most fundamental issue in starting relationships is trust. It is the sine qua non of any human relationship. There is no other place to start. Time and again, I have listened to brokenhearted people who have told me they thought they could trust the other person. Perhaps it was an unfaithful spouse, perhaps a child who stole, a boss who was cruel, or a parent who was evil. The heart of each of these persons was weighted down by betrayal. The trust was broken, and without trust, there could be no helpful interchanges.

Trust has two basic parts: predictable behavior and similar values. Predictable behavior means that 85–90 percent of the time you can predict the other person's behavior. What the person says he or she will do, the person does. If your boyfriend says that he will pick you up for work each morning at 8:00 A.M., and in fact, is there most mornings at 8:00 A.M., then you can predict his behavior. But what are you to do if he is one hour late one morning? You listen for his explanation. Was there a traffic jam? Did the battery go dead? If the explanation is reasonable, *and* he continues to be on time, then his behavior remains predictable. Words and actions need to match 85–90 percent of the time. Because life is complicated and at times beyond our control, a 10–15 percent margin for error is to be expected. If the words and actions do not match, always choose to believe the person's behavior. Behavior has been around much longer than language. You can never trust someone whose behavior you cannot predict.

Caring Attachments Require Continuous Communication.

"Do you want to talk about it?"

If the person's behavior is reasonably predictable, then move to the second part: similar values. As we noted earlier, basic value conflicts are harmful types of exchanges. Do you and this person whose behavior is predictable have generally similar values? Do you both value life, honesty, and caring for others? Do you both value theft, murder, and fraud? To continue with our example, when your boyfriend predictably picks you up at 8:00 A.M., does he drive safely as you would? Does he verbally denigrate you all the way to work in a manner you would not do to him? Are you always paying for the gasoline and parking? His behavior is predictable, but do you have similar values? Trust is never guess work, never solely a "feeling." It is a matter of observation and thought: is the person's behavior generally predictable? Do we have similar values?

When you meet someone for the first time, you cannot really trust or mistrust the other person. Time needs to pass so that you can see if the other person's behavior is predictable and whether you both have similar values. Trust never need be guesswork.

Sustaining Relationships. What are the leading causes of divorce in our country? Consumer debt, infidelity, and alcoholism. From these facts, it is clear that relationships that start in trust and with mutual sharing may come upon hard times without continuous work, communication, and nourishment. Since the second half of this book focuses on how to sustain attachments, I will only note the issues here in a general way.

Communication is first and foremost. It sounds like a truism, but for any of us who do couples' counseling, it is clear that the longer people are together, the more they *assume* they know what the other person is thinking. Not necessarily so. The world is complex, the people in it change, and you will never know of the changes without continuous communication. Couples need to set aside time each day to talk with each other about their life together in our complex technological age.

In Maslow's hierarchy of needs, for relationships to be sustained, each party must have their various needs addressed. Physiological and safety needs (e.g., food, clothing, shelter), to be sure, have to be met, but as relationships lengthen, social and esteem needs are usually of greater importance because by then safety is usually a given. People in relationships need to care about each other and employ the helpful relationship skills outlined in this chapter.

If you are afraid of losing control in relationships or fear being harmed by others, if you feel too emotionally drained to help others, or if you hate to conform to the generally accepted rules for relationships, professional counseling will probably be of help. In my professional experience, these issues keep people from really caring about each other and are hard to overcome without some professional counseling.

Closely related to caring about each other is the role of money in relationships. Human encounters that are overwhelmed with material goods and/or staggering debt are ready prey for disruption. One of my colleagues recently referred a couple to me for marriage counseling. They were constantly arguing about their sexual incompatibility, and came to me for advice. Knowing that sexual dysfunction can often be a result of too much stress, I inquired about their financial circumstances. They had a combined income of thirty-five thousand dollars and credit card debt of eleven thousand dollars. Not car payments. Not mortgage payments. Credit-card debt only. Relationships that are preoccupied with money leave little time or energy for the caring and nourishing needed by the persons in that relationship.

Ending Relationships. One of my patients once told me that she thought of life as a series of comings and goings. There is much truth in her statement. One of the painful parts of being human is knowing that everything that is physically human will come to an end. All our joys, and pleasures, and happinesses on earth will end. Death is a part of life. Death is the final ending, but we experience other endings and other losses before we die. The loss of housing, the loss of employment, the loss of health, separation from loved ones, each of these is an ending, a life stress to which we must respond. These losses are the source of much life stress. The leave-taking creates separation anxiety, and the process of coping with this event is called grieving.

Separation anxiety is most commonly seen in little children. What happens when the mother leaves the infant? What does the baby do? Its stress response is activated, it feels itself in turmoil, it cries and calls for the mother to return. The baby is saying: do not leave me, do not separate, do not go away, I need you here with me. Adults go through similar feelings when they must say good-bye.

Dr. Elisabeth Kübler-Ross (1969) has taught us much about the grieving process. It includes a natural progression of five steps for the dying person and often the family members and loved ones as well. *Denial* is the first stage. The person refuses to believe the event is happening. In the case of death, the patient may refuse to believe the truth of the medical findings. The second stage involves *anger*. The person now realizes the diagnosis is correct but becomes angry with the realization that his or her aspirations and hopes will not be realized. *Bargaining* comes next as the person barters with God for extra time to do things. This is followed by *depression* as the person realizes that time is drawing to a close. The fifth stage is *acceptance* when the person is at peace with dying. These stages are similar for other types of losses as well.

We have seen now how stress-resistant persons utilize reasonable mastery and caring attachments to mitigate the potential negative impact of life stress. Stress-resistant people further enhance their capacities to cope by paying close attention to what their bodies and the world about them tell them about the presence and impact of life stress.

We likewise can increase our stress resistance by furthering our understanding of these processes. Toward that end, we will examine the physiology of stress in the next chapter, and the factors in our society that activate the stress response in chapter 4. A full awareness of these two factors will enhance our ability to choose the right stress management strategy for any particular problem that we may encounter. Such an awareness augments our ability to understand the events going on about us so that we can use our skills at reasonable mastery and caring attachments with more precise effectiveness.

3

STRESS AND BURNOUT: WHEN MASTERY AND ATTACHMENT FAIL

Tempus fugit.
—Ovid

The proper function of man is to live, not to exist.
—Jack London

She snapped at him as he came down the stairs from the bedroom. "Will you pick up after yourself? You're as bad as the kids." She fought back the tears. Did he understand? He nodded politely as he ambled out the kitchen door to his left. Nothing ever seemed to faze him.

Pudgy. Overweight actually. Mirrors were unremittingly clear that way. Was she eating her way through the anxiety or the depression? No time for that now. Anne had rushed upstairs to dress for work herself. She was going to be late for her bus.

Certainly, part of her anxiety was in just dealing with all the changes. In her day, a secretary typed, cut stencils, and did some filing during slack times. Now she had to master word processors, fax machines, software, floppy discs. User friendly, the manuals had said. Downright hostile had been her experience.

She wondered if her Kit had been like these younger women in the office. Preoccupied by success and money, power, and sex. Everything was at once so casual and so fast-paced.

She thought about her own joy just a short year ago. She and Kit, her youngest, had spent the whole year planning. The church, the dress, the hall and caterer, the guest list. How busy and fulfilled she had seemed then. Now in the six months since Kit had married, the whole bottom had fallen out of her life. Years of getting the kids to ballet or hockey practice, nursing sore throats, doing multiplication tables. Her life, her role, the parental expectations that had been so clear for her were as absent as her children.

Forty-six year old Jessica stood confronting reentry into the paid labor force. Traffic, technology, relentless deadlines. Was she angry? Probably. Was she saddened? Likely. Was she bitter? Possibly. Was she depressed? All the time. No one had prepared her for the "empty nest." What was to become of her? Did fathers feel this way or only mothers? Would today's young working mothers have the same distress when they turned forty, or would their continuous employment buffer them?

As the doors of the bus hissed open, she fumbled for the exact change. It would be nice, she thought, if life's problems had the equivalent of exact change solutions. As she sat down and was jostled by the woman next to her, the bus pulled away on her adventure to nowhere. The confusion was nerve-racking.

Here is a common example of life stress. This woman has given over two decades of her life and many of her best years in attending to the rearing of her children. Now within a few short months, her skills at reasonable mastery and her caring attachments have been so severed that she is both intensely anxious and depressed. Her physiology of stress has been activated by an important cultural shift in her role in life. She is attempting to move from full-time parent to full-time paid employee. Similar shifts can and do happen to all of us.

Life is often not fair, and change is inevitable anyway so we, along with Jessica, are well-advised to understand what stress is and how it comes about. Let us begin with what happens to us when we are under stress, and particularly, what happens to us biologically.

What Is Stress?

Stress is the state of discomfort that arises when our problems exceed our resources to cope with them (Lazarus and Folkman, 1984). If you owe a hundred dollars, the other party wants the hundred dollars, and you do not have the hundred dollars, your problem has exceeded your resources. Stress is present until the problem is solved, and illness may follow if the problem remains unremedied for too long.

Stressful situations befall all of us in life as we have seen in our examples. Some are biological (extreme heat or cold); some are psychological (rejection, loss of self-esteem). Others are sociological (schooling, unemployment) or philosophical (what are the values or meaning of life). Table 1 presents some common stressful events as well as some of the medical problems that can arise if such events are not dealt with. It is currently estimated that 75 percent of all illnesses are stress-related.

The contents of table 1 raise many questions for all of us concerned with stress. Given our definition of stress, how do any of the events in the left-hand column actually come to be associated with any of the mind and body diseases in the right-hand column? Why are the events on the left stressful for some persons but not for others? Are there some factors or coping strategies that will mitigate the impact of such events? Why does the stress of life seem worse in the eighties? How would I know if I was not coping well?

Table 1

Common Stressful Situations and Common Stress-related Diseases:

STRESSFUL SITUATIONS	STRESS-RELATED DISEASES
Death of a Loved One	Heart Disease
Unemployment	Some Types of Cancer
Divorce	Anxiety
Owing Money	Depression
Problems at Work or at Home	Suicide
Pregnancy and Child Rearing	Alcohol Abuse
Schooling	Drug Abuse
Driving in Traffic	Major and Minor Accidents
Retirement	with Injury
	Psychosomatic Diseases
	including some Ulcer,
	Spastic Colon,
	Respiratory and Skin
	Disorders

Are there any early telltale signs before I would get really sick? Is there any way to get a handle on my life?

These are very important questions, and I encourage you to spend some time thinking about them. The pace of our daily life is such that we rarely take the time to reflect on these basic questions. We are moving so quickly that it never occurs to us to even think about such basic questions. Yet, like Jessica, we too may suddenly find ourselves confronted by these questions. Understanding these questions will increase our capacity to manage stress. For example, can you explain to yourself why you recently had your last bout with the common cold? Since such germs are always in our environment, what was it that specifically caused you to get sick that last time? Why on that day and not the next day? How would Dr. Hinkle help you answer this question?

Let me begin by answering one of the most basic questions first: What is our goal in managing stress? We manage stress to preserve our physical and mental health, and to attain a sense of well-being. Without these, life becomes boring, miserable, and even painful. None of us is always free from illness and/or unhappiness, but good practices for coping with stress can reduce the frequency of such negative states.

Without stress management strategies we will have increasing anxiety, depression, physical illness, and/or even premature death. It is important to clearly understand why so many of us in today's world feel overwhelmed and unable to catch up with the demands placed upon us.

The Fundamental Cause of Too Much Stress

As we have seen, reasonable mastery and good human relationships or attachments are the key resources for stress resistance. Since these are potentially available in abundance in our society, the root of the problem must lie elsewhere. There must be some factor in our daily lives that keeps us from sound mastery and meaningful attachments. I think the offender is hidden in one of our basic cultural values—more precisely an excessive pursuit of this value.

We are all encouraged to pursue the American Dream: to strive for maximum personal achievement, and the greatest amount of material goods that we can attain. We are encouraged to "have it all." Given the deprivation of the Great Depression of the 1930s, and the world war of the 1940s, it should not surprise us that, as a people, we should want better times. Given our ingenuity, it should also not surprise us that we have succeeded in producing beyond anyone's dreams in the history of civilization—a society with a vast array of material goods and avenues for personal achievement. Herein lies the problem.

Moderate pursuit of these goals is reasonable and beneficial to health and well-being. However, as we shall see, there are now so many opportunities that none of us has the physical energy, or time, or money to "have it all." More importantly, the pursuit of material goods and personal individual achievement is drawing us further and further away from others, from the meaningful human attachments that are crucial to reducing stress as we have seen. This excessive pursuit of the goals of the American Dream is increasing our stress, taxing the capacity of our bodies to respond, and leading to demoralization, illness, and often premature death. We're overdoing a good thing, and we're paying a great price for doing so.

As our technological advances increase, as our expectations increase, and as our personal, corporate, and national debt increase, we can only look forward to the harried stress of life increasing also. There are things we can do to have the best of both possible worlds (mastery and attachments), but we need to fully understand that at the moment we are pursuing mastery at the expense of attachments. We are not developing the skills of stress-resistant persons.

Our preoccupation with the automobile clearly represents our predicaments as a society. The car symbolizes individual freedom and personal mobility in a self-contained environment. Our involvement with others is detached. We share the same roadway and sit in the same traffic jams; but in these new wagon trains, we sit alone, cut off from each other. The car, like much of technology, isolates us from each other.

It needn't be this way. None of us can "have it all" for the reasons I have noted: there is not enough physical energy, time, or money, with the result that we often have fewer caring attachments to others. We can have some of the good life, maybe even much of it over time, but none of us can have it all at once. This is the strength of stress-resistant people. They realize that none of us can have it all, and they find a balance between reasonable mastery and caring attachments so that their lives are happy and productive. We can do likewise.

The unexamined life is not only not worth living, but it usually is full of stress. Leave yourself time to think about your values and your goals, your needs and wants. Since none of us can "have it all," this implies choices, and good choices presuppose serious reflection.

Assessing Your Stress/Illness Potential

Most disease is the result of multiple risk factors, and we need to be mindful of this.

George Albee (1980), a psychologist, has presented a beginners' guide for help in assessing some of the risks in becoming sick from life stress:

$$\text{Health/Illness} = \frac{\text{Biological Limitations} \times \text{Stressful Life Events}}{\text{Coping Resources} \times \text{Social Supports}}$$

The first of his four factors is biological limitations. These limitations refer to physical incapacities present at birth or resulting from bodily injury after birth. We have noted how limitations such as poor hearing or vision, cerebral palsy, mental retardation, spinal injury, and the like are all medical limitations that make coping with life stress more difficult because the limitation itself reduces our capacity to respond fully.

The second factor is the array of stressful life events such as those in table 1 and in the examples I have given. Stressful life events can include the predictable problems of normal human development as well as unpredictable events such as natural disasters like earthquakes and floods, and man-made disasters such as terrorism or nuclear accidents.

Coping resources and social supports are the helpful factors, those events that can mitigate or lessen the negative impact of biological limitations and stressful life events. These two factors may lessen the probability of becoming ill. Coping resources, the third factor, are those tools that give us reasonable control over our environment so that we can attain what we need and want. Such resources are our attempts at reasonable mastery. Some resources are material goods: central heating and air-conditioning, refrigerators, indoor lighting, and plumbing. Each of these resources helps us to cope with potentially stressful life events. Other coping resources are psychological, and include skills such as problem solving, making one's own decisions, and organizing tasks and time. These complicated coping resources are most frequently referred to as mastery, the term I am employing in this book.

The fourth factor is social supports or attachments. These are the meaningful relationships we have with other human beings. As we have seen, medical science and stress-resistant persons know that beneficial attachments can provide both psychological as well as physiological help in reducing stress. Helpful advice, a helping hand, or a shoulder to lean on are examples of such beneficial attachments. Likewise, they also know that harmful relationships can be a nuisance or even potentially damaging, such as another person being overly demanding or emotionally self-centered.

Note that in Dr. Albee's guide for health we find again the central theme of this book: one copes with both reasonable mastery and good attachments. We need both to function at our best. We need both to become stress-resistant.

You are now able to make an initial assessment of your current potential risk for stress-related disease. What, if any, are the biological limitations that you need to be mindful of? What are the current problems in your life? What is the nature and extent of your mastery skills and your helpful human attachments? Do you want it all or have you found a reasonable balance between mastery and attachment? What is your current risk for getting sick? If you are not feeling well now, you already know the answer. All of us need to gauge our risk factors as best we can. I have included a series of questionnaires in appendix A to help you with this self-assessment. While these questionnaires have scientific limitations, they can still be helpful beginning guides. How to score these questionnaires and what your scores mean may be found there also.

The Basic Process for Coping with Life Stress

Now that we know what stress is, and why it comes about, we need to understand how the human mind and body have been created to respond to it effectively.

Do You Sometimes Feel Overwhelmed By Life Stress?

"I'm ready, dear!"

Élan Vital. Élan vital is a French expression that means "vital living force." Since medical science doesn't fully know what biological life is, I find it helpful to think of élan vital as a simile in the following way: I use élan vital to refer to the biological energy that makes us functioning human beings. The amount of élan vital that each of us has is fixed at conception. From that point on, as we live and breathe, we are using up our reserves of élan vital. None of us ever gets any more than what we have at conception. If longevity runs in your family, you may have a bit more élan vital to start with; however, for all of us our fixed amount is continually being depleted. When it is fully gone, we are biologically dead.

The goal of stress resistance is to utilize our élan vital wisely so that we maintain our health and sense of well-being.

Continuing with our élan vital simile, the stress of life wastes élan vital, uses it up faster than need be, and can leave us sick and even shorten our life span. The poor use of élan vital keeps us from the health and well-being that we seek. There is evidence, however, that we can exert some reasonable control over how quickly this élan vital is used up. The average human could live for about 110 years, yet most of us are often sick and die between the ages of seventy-five and seventy-eight. While women traditionally have lived longer than men, their longevity edge appears to be declining. In fact, in the 1970s women's health began to fail at a rate more similar to men's health (Barnett, Biener, and Baruch, 1987). Clearly, many of us are not managing our stress well if both men and women are dying thirty years earlier than we seem genetically programmed to do.

Nature has provided us with a feedback system that tells us if we are managing the stress of life in adequate ways that preserve our élan vital.

If we are managing stress effectively, our élan vital is utilized wisely and conservatively, and we would know if this were so because we would have good physical and mental health, and the sense of well-being that we have spoken of.

Good health is the general absence of mental distress and physical disease. If you are generally free from incapacitating anxiety and depression, major illnesses, or frequent accidents, then you are in good health. Well-being is more than the absence of disease. It is a sense of contentment, inner peace, basic happiness, and an excitement about being alive. If you have good health and a sense of well-being, your mind and your body are telling you that you are using your élan vital wisely.

The messages of poor utilization and distress are equally clear: the loss of the sense of well-being, followed by anxiety and depression, and physical illnesses. If we choose to ignore these messages over several months and years, a shortened life span and premature death are likely possible outcomes. Any of these negative messages tells us immediately that we are wasting our élan vital, and, by inference, are using poor strategies for managing stress.

It is important to remember that we can exercise some control over how our élan vital is used. We cannot prevent ourselves from ever becoming sick, but by the judicious use of reasonable mastery and good attachments to others we can keep distress to a minimum.

The Coping Process. How does stress make us sick? How does it squander our élan vital? How do events outside our bodies cause disease inside our bodies?

The basic steps in the coping process are presented in figure 1. The potentially stressful situations of step 1, figure 1 we have already spoken of. These include the physical, psychological, social, and existential problems that befall us as individuals and groups. These are listed as *potentially* stressful because the quality of our coping response determines whether or not there will be negative health consequences.

Listed also are people demands that can be a special form of potential stress. While people may be helpful in reducing stress as we have noted, there is an important exception to this rule. Individuals who provide services to others are frequently receiving demands from those they serve. Professionals such as teachers, police officers, managers, nurses, secretaries, and mothers often have excessive demands made of them, and such people demands produce stress plus a special form of people stress called burnout (see step 3).

The person who must cope with the stressful situations is repre-

Figure 1

How Stress Occurs:

Step 1	*Step 2*
1. Potentially stressful situations ↔	The Coping Person →
2. People Demands	(With Both Mind and Body)
	1. Homeostasis
	2. Circadian Rhythm
	3. General Adaptation Syndrome
	4. Cognitive Appraisal
Step 3	*Step 4*
Stress Response ↑ ↓	→ Poor Solutions
And Burnout	Worry
	Learned Helplessness
4. Perceived Threat	
3. Immune, Endorphin, Sex	
2. Adrenalin	
1. Muscles	

sented in step 2. All of us cope with our minds and our bodies. The first is obvious: we have a problem, we think about how to solve it, we implement a strategy and evaluate whether it works or not.

What many of us do not realize is that our bodies can also be a helpful tool in coping with life stress. Good physical health and sound conditioning can mitigate the negative impact of many stressful events. Conversely, poor physical conditioning can increase the stress we must respond to. We need to work in harmony with our natural body processes for responding to stress.

The first special process is referred to as homeostasis (Cannon, 1963). This is the body's own internal system for balancing or regulating a part of the body known as the autonomic nervous system. This system oversees processes like heart rate, blood pressure, and breathing. When the body has to cope with stress, it sounds an alarm. The autonomic system increases heart rate, muscle tone, and mental alertness; the result is that élan vital is utilized intensely. When the stress has been resolved, the automatic system returns the body to its homeostatic resting state, and élan vital is preserved. This system is involuntary—it works automatically without the body and brain consciously willing it. Effective coping strategies, however, can aid in returning the body to its natural homeostasis as quickly as possible.

The second special process is called circadian rhythm, and refers to a second automatic bodily process. It is the body's twenty-four-hour internal clock. This body clock regulates the daily rhythms of the body such as the sleep/wake cycle, necessary changes in body chemistry, metabolism or the burning of energy, and the like. Every morning when you open your eyes, the biological clock that is near the visual system automatically resets itself for another twenty-four hour period. If your daily life conforms to this internal clock's rhythms, your élan vital is utilized most efficiently. If your daily routine disrupts the clock's timing, however, élan vital is wasted. Jet lag is the circadian rhythm disruption most of us are familiar with. When we change time zones, the sun rises earlier or later than our "hometown" time base, and our rhythm is no longer synchronized. Constantly changing shifts at work is another common disruption for many manufacturing and service persons, since their hours for sleeping are continually being altered in relation to sunrise. It is best to plan your life to your body's clock rhythms.

The third special process is the general adaptation syndrome

(Selye, 1956). The body has its own internal three-stage process for responding to stress. The first stage is the alarm or readiness phase where the incoming messages to the brain make the brain focus its attention on the impending stressful life event that it has confronted. In the second stage, the brain resists or works actively to solve the problem before entering the third or recovery stage where the body restores its energy and homeostasis for the next problem that comes its way. Again, this process, like homeostasis and circadian rhythm, is automatic: readiness, resistance, recovery. Our élan vital is best utilized by allowing our bodies to go through the three stages of the general adaptation syndrome. In our culture, however, we rarely allow the time our bodies need to rest and recover. Even when stress has led to disease, even then when our bodies are clearly telling us to rest and recover, we get up out of bed and go to work when we have the flu.

The fourth and last special process occurs during the problem-solving second stage of the general adaptation syndrome. This process is a two-step cognitive evaluation of the stressful event (Lazarus and Folkman, 1984). The brain gives meaning to the stressful event by making two appraisals instantly: "Is this a serious problem or not?" and "What can be done to cope?" These appraisals are drawn from current experience as well as similar experiences the brain has interpreted from past events. An event that is assigned as threat, fear, anxiety, anger, or boredom becomes a stressful event. It is in this process that the potentially stressful events in figure 1 are actually determined as stressful or not. Similarly, an event that is considered benign or helpful remains a nonstressful event.

Let us review what we know about the coping person in the second step of figure 1. The coping person's goal is to use as little unnecessary élan vital as possible in coping with life stress. The coping person will make best use of both his or her mind and body. This person will attempt to solve problems quickly to maintain homeostasis, and will conduct his/her daily routine in accordance with the body's circadian rhythm. This person who is coping adequately will also remember the necessary phases of readiness, resistance, and recovery, and will pay attention to the process of appraisal. If the coping person allows these natural processes to occur, what is called the stress response will be used efficiently without wasting élan vital.

Return now to figure 1, and step 3: the Stress Response. The stress response refers to the physiological manner in which our bodies respond when we are confronted with stressful life events. The physiology of stress arousal is a very complicated process. For example, there are thousands of changes just in brain chemistry alone each moment. Yet in spite of this complexity, most people find it helpful to have at least some rudimentary sense of what is happening internally when they are feeling overwhelmed.

There are at least four interlocking components: (1) Our muscles tighten up. We have well over 700 muscles in our bodies that we can control (e.g., moving our arms, moving our jaws), and under stress they become poised to help us respond. (2) Adrenalin begins to flow. Adrenalin increases blood pressure, and breathing, and helps to focus our attention on the problem at hand. (3) The systems in our bodies that maintain our sense of well-being function less efficiently. Our immune system that fights certain types of diseases works less well. (This is one reason why people may become ill when under stress.) Our endorphins, the chemicals in our brains that make us feel good, circulate less. Our interest in sex also wanes under stress. (4) Finally, our brain perceives the threat and focuses on the potential harm. All of these components interact with each other. Thus, when one is activated, the other three are activated within seconds.

Imagine yourself confronted by an angry bear. Your muscles tighten up so that you can run, if need be; your adrenalin pumps so that you are operating at peak efficiency; and your systems for well-being are less active so that you can focus your full attention on the bear. (The last things on your mind should be worries about catching a cold, being mellow when you meet the bear, or having your attention distracted by one of the beautiful people.) The components of the stress response are activated to help you cope, to help you stay alive. These four components are the body's basic response to stress.

You will remember back in step 1 that people demands were a special form of potential stress. For individuals providing service to others, there are two further components to the stress response in addition to the four we have mentioned so far. If the demands of others are too great, not only will the stress response be activated, but the service providers will additionally find themselves physically and psychologically withdrawing from those whom they seek to help. Further, they will then begin to denigrate these same people (from a teacher—"All students cheat"; from a lawyer—"All citizens are crooks"). When a person is overwhelmed by too many taxing demands from other people, he or she may develop burnout. Burnout is the special form of stress that may result from helping others who make demands. Burnout includes not only the four components of the stress response for general problems, but also the extra components of withdrawal and denigration. It is reversible through good stress management practices.

The role of the stress response is to ensure our survival in a crisis. Notice the arrows to the left of step 3. These arrows indicate that it is normal for the stress response to go on and off. In a crisis, it goes on immediately, prepares us for the crisis, and burns our élan vital vigorously. When the crisis has passed, it shuts off and returns our bodies to a quiet phase by means of homeostasis. Élan vital is now preserved and utilized much more gradually. This process is much like a light switch. Stress response: on/off. Élan vital: on/off.

Since the stress response ensures survival, we speak of coping with stress, not eliminating it. If we eliminated the stress response completely, our mechanisms for self-protection would all be gone, and we would soon be dead. Presumably, this is not exactly the outcome that you are seeking from your strategies for coping with stress.

While it is clear that we don't want to eliminate the stress response, it is equally clear that we want to solve our problem, and return the body to its normal resting state to preserve our élan vital. As long as the stress response is on, we are using up extra élan vital and running the risk of demoralization, illness, and even premature death. As we shall learn in the next chapter, there are forces in our culture as well as patterns in our daily lives that keep the stress response on even when there are no life threatening consequences. Our culture encourages us to have it all. Such emphases are unfortunate because they may waste élan vital, and the fundamental goal in all stress management is to preserve élan vital so that we will have health and well-being.

Step 4 of figure 1 presents those processes that will keep the physiology of the stress response in overdrive. They do so because by their very nature they preclude an adaptive solution to coping with stressful life events, and it is adaptive solutions that permit the stress response to tone down and return to a more normal resting state. Poor solutions, worry, and learned helplessness are common examples of maladaptive coping strategies.

Poor solutions are those that leave the problem unsolved. The problem at hand needs to be addressed. Focus on the true problem, do not assign unnecessary meanings of harm, gather the necessary resources to cope, implement a solution. Do not put the problem off, especially if it will preoccupy your mind. Many of us regularly do not follow these simple steps. We hope the problems will somehow go away. Usually they do not, and in the meantime, our physiology is in overdrive, and our élan vital is being wasted.

Worry is a second factor in stress response overdrive. As we have noted, the four components of the basic stress response interact with each other so that, if you are perfectly calm and begin to worry (perceived threat), all the other components of the stress response are immediately activated. This is why worriers have trouble falling asleep. Their bodies are wide-awake. For example, if someone is worrying about work, he or she might as well be at the office and working on the problem he or she is worrying about. Mental worrying is the same as actually being there in terms of your stress response. People worry even when there is no problem. They worry about not being as good the next time. (I once had a patient I instructed not to worry just for one week. A week later she told me she had generally done well except for Sunday afternoon when she began to worry about what she would do if she began to worry!) Aerobic exercise (swimming, jogging) prevents undue worry, and we will see the reason for this shortly.

Learned helplessness is the third factor in stress response overdrive. When some individuals encounter *one* potentially life-threatening problem that they cannot solve, they sometimes make a false assumption that they won't be able to do much about their other problems either. They learn to be helpless when in fact they are not so. Even more unfortunate is their next assumption that no one else (ministers, spouse, friends, therapists) can help them either. This is a special (but treatable) problem that we shall discuss in detail later.

Let us briefly summarize. Stressful life events may befall us. As we encounter these potentially stressful situations, and cope with our minds and bodies, we want our stress response to go off and remain off as quickly as possible in each case. This is normal and preserves élan vital. If the stress response remains in overdrive, important élan vital reserves are being put in action. Should the overdrive condition continue, demoralization, anxiety and depression, physical illnesses, and even premature death may follow. We manage stress, we cannot eliminate it. The reason for managing it should hopefully now be clear to you. It really is a matter of life or death.

Left Brain/Right Brain. Just as nature has given us the stress response to automatically protect us, nature has also provided a ready response to shut it off when the crisis has passed. Nature's secret is your right brain.

The highest centers of the human brain are known as the cortex, and this cortex is divided into two spheres. The half to your left, the left brain is used mainly for language, thinking, reasoning (and worry). The part of your brain to your right, the right brain, is used mainly for the visual and spatial locomotion of your body in the environment. Right brain allows you to walk, run, dance, and so forth without bumping into things. As you read this book, you are using your left brain. As you walked to your desk to read this book, you were using your right brain.

We know that the brain is more complicated than this, and that some of these functions overlap, but it is still true that a number of activities primarily associated with right brain activity appear to shut off the stress response in many people. Some of the more common include: aerobic exercise; walking; relaxation exercises; biofeedback; prayer and meditation; humor and crying; art, music, and dance; and certain hobbies like photography.

The advantage of a right-brain activity in managing stress is that it shuts off all four components of the stress response at the same time. You will remember that activating one component of the stress response activates the other three, so that the most effective strategy for stress management is to shut the whole process off at once. This is why medicines like the minor tranquilizers are usually weak long-term strategies for coping with stress. They produce habituation (and often dependency) and they do not address the life stress that is producing the stress response. Right brain activities are far more effective, and should be used by each of us.

This is especially true for people who worry. There is increasing evidence that worriers are probably born this way, but that hard exercise will effectively take the edge off of the worrying. The problem will be there to solve, but the worrier won't be obsessed and fret about it. When I counsel worriers, one homework assignment I give them is to swim a few laps or jog a few blocks and try to worry themselves into turmoil. They report back (with relief) that they were able to think about the issue, but were unable to work themselves into emotional turmoil. They also think I am one smart counselor, but right brain deserves the credit.

Using right-brain activities thus becomes a central strategy in an overall stress reduction program. Which ones on the list do you already use? Which ones would interest you? The good thing about these right-brain activities is that nature will not let your brain be tripped up in the face of a true life-threatening situation. In the case of a true crisis, Nature protects you with an activated stress response, and your brain cannot switch to right-brain stress reduction strategies. Thus, if you feel you are in stress overdrive when there is no true life-threatening crisis, a right brain activity is a useful first step in reducing stress and conserving élan vital. (If you are over thirty-five or have been ill, see your physician before you start an aerobic exercise task.)

Now that we have a general sense of what stress is and the processes that are activated within us when we are confronted with life's problems, we need to examine more fully our national pursuit of "having it all." As we noted in passing earlier in the chapter, attempting to "have it all" places our stress response in overdrive. We push ourselves even when there is no immediate life-threatening crisis. This desire to achieve and acquire more and more in less and less time wastes élan vital unnecessarily. A clearer understanding of this cultural value that seems to drive us on so relentlessly will provide us with a perspective on the age in which we live. Such a perspective will enhance our capacity for stress resistance by enabling us to make the best life choices from the many options before all of us. It will facilitate our finding the helpful balance between reasonable mastery and caring attachments.

4

THE RAT RACE: THE CULTURAL SOURCES OF STRESS

Nearly every American hungers to move.
—John Steinbeck

. . . the knowledge of science for the needs of man.
—Auguste Comte

With sirens and lights ablaze, Rescue One sped towards the hospital's emergency room. In the rear of the truck in cramped and sterile quarters, EMT Rosario worked silently to keep the heart of Henry Abbott Wallace from stopping. The odds of such success were bleak. Mr. Wallace, the "never-say-die" competitor, was inches from death. For one of the few times in his life, Henry Wallace was frightened. He was terrified, to be more precise, of the crushing pain in his chest. He had just turned forty-one two weeks earlier.

Henry was the corporate craftsman. He worked long, long hours into the night, was fiercely competitive, and rarely at rest. He did everything himself, and his sense of urgency was palpable. It was not uncommon to see him talking on the phone and to his secretary alternately, writing himself a memo, and gulping coffee all at the same time. His hostility, when he was interrupted, was a legend in the office. He "relaxed" once a week by playing tennis with a business associate. His staff referred to this weekly event as the Battle of Armageddon.

The emergency room staff worked quickly, quietly, efficiently in the bright white lighting of the room. Dr. Wilson knew that the patient on the table before him was truly near death. Oxygen, IV drops, medicines. With militarylike precision the ER team implemented the procedure to save a human life. With three hours of concentrated effort, the patient had responded. Mr. Wallace's heart rate, blood pressure, and pulse were reasonably stable. He was wheeled to the Intensive Care Unit; and through the darkness of that long first night, Mr. Wallace's vital signs remained stable.

At eleven o'clock the next morning, Mr. Wallace's monitors shrieked their alarm. His vital signs were again in chaos; the crushing pain, again his adversary. Wilson and his staff worked feverishly to save their patient yet again.

What had happened? The nursing charts noted that Mr. Wallace had had a female visitor one half-hour before his second cardiac arrest. Who was this femme fatale? Was it his wife? Was it his mistress? It proved to be his secretary. Mr. Wallace had been dictating office correspondence in the ICU. Time was money. Even in death, he could not stop.

Mr. Wallace is a driven man. In many ways he is the prototype of "success" in our culture. He wants it all. Hard working, devoted to the company, and to increased earnings, he represents the best of our corporate world, and, unfortunately, the ill health that may result from the worst of its excesses.

Not all of us push to the extreme that Mr. Wallace does, but in our own not-so-obvious ways we are also impatient. Our driver behavior at red lights offers some illustrative examples.

Since today's average motorist spends six months of his/her life sitting at traffic lights, my students and I decided to observe driver behavior at the lights. Traffic lights on average change every sixty seconds, and the vehicle, if it is not driven carefully, is a potentially lethal weapon. You might expect that the stressed and overburdened drivers would use that sixty seconds to rest and compose their thoughts. It is a *mere sixty* seconds, after all. Here is what we observed.

Drivers engage in various acts of personal hygiene: shaving, combing hair, putting on makeup, polishing nails, and brushing teeth with the window rolled up. (This last one was of particular interest, but the light changed so we'll never know how this person solved that problem.) Drivers also spend a lot of time eating: they have breakfast in plastic containers on the dashboard, lunches in paper wrappers, and dinner and snacks in a variety of assorted cartons. Drivers also work at traffic lights: they have car phones, portable lap word processors, audio cassettes on how to succeed in business, and an infinite variety of books, journals, newspapers, and magazines. Many drivers work hard to refine their skills in being rude. They sneer, yell, honk, flash high-beams, deliberately go slowly, and make vulgar gestures with their arms and fingers. (We even found one driver praying—possibly after observing these other drivers.) Finally, and of great concern, drivers do drugs and alcohol at traffic lights. Sometimes this abuse starts in the early daylight hours so that, by midafternoon, many of these drivers are physically unable to operate the vehicle. (State troopers confirm that all of these behaviors have also been noted at seventy miles per hour when the driver has only one hand on the wheel.)

Some of this behavior is funny, much of it is dangerous. The more basic question, however, is why is it happening at all? Why are these drivers as restless, as compelled as Mr. Wallace, our cardiac competitor with death? We are talking about sixty seconds. If we review the driver behavior, we find people grooming, eating, working, and reading. These tasks used to be called daily living, and they occurred at home and at one's work site. Now daily living seems to be occurring behind the steering wheel of a car or truck. Equally distressing is the callousness with which we treat others. We see rudeness, hostility, selfishness.

The question is why? Why are we driven so relentlessly? Why have we become preoccupied with material success to the exclusion of caring for others? For a society that prides itself on personal control, why do things often feel as if they are becoming unraveled? Is it just human nature? Has it always been this way? Is it worse now? Let us keep these questions in mind as we examine three societies in human history.

Three Societies

There have been some remarkable and profound changes in human history in the past forty thousand years. These shifts have been very basic and impact on the way we live our daily lives centuries later. Since most of us find our energies focused on our immediate problems, we often neglect to pay attention to the more fundamental changes. Yet, suggestions for coping with stress will be of limited value if we do not understand the basic values and forces in culture that inform our daily tasks. These lessons from history are important for informed choice and for longer-term planning to reduce stress. Toward that end, we need to understand three major periods in the history of the human family: the hunter/gathering peoples, the agricultural/farming peoples, and our own industrial/corporate age.

Our review actually begins at least forty thousand years ago. By that time in the history of the evolution of the human family, the internal physiology of the human body was fixed and established as we know it today. This means that our central nervous system, our autonomic system, and our general basic body structure were essentially formed. Our stress response (for survival), homeostasis, circadian rhythm, general adaptation syndrome, and cognitive processes for assigning meaning to events were also in place to allow the human organism to cope and adapt successfully to its environment. There have been no fundamental shifts in our basic biological makeup since then.

Our bodily processes to cope with stress thus were adapted to an environment and a life-style that existed forty thousand years ago. This is the first lesson in history that we should consider. The world that we live in today, as we shall see, is very different from the world our internal body chemistry was built to respond to. While it is true that evolution continues, it is also true that any significant change in our environment and our daily life-style requires tens of thousands of years for the body to adapt to such a change. As we shall learn, our lives in the twentieth century have had to undergo two such basic shifts in less than one twelve-thousand-year period: the shift to farming and then to industrial life. Thus, in the most fundamental of ways, you and I are coping with evolutionary shifts for which our minds and bodies needed many tens-of-thousand-year periods rather than one twelve-thousand-year period. It should not surprise us that we are having problems managing stress. It should not surprise us that we feel overwhelmed. Nor should it surprise us that we are having trouble putting our finger on the basic problem. It is a subtle lesson from history, seemingly far removed from the immediacy of today's evening commute in rush hour traffic, but it is an important lesson. This first lesson from history is that the basic shifts in our culture that have evolved so quickly and the traffic jams of life are not unrelated. The human family hasn't had time to adjust.

An equally important lesson from history is that there are still helpful ways to cope and adapt even in the face of these fundamental shifts in our environment. Some of the effective strategies for coping that could be helpful to us in our own century were actually utilized by our ancestors, the hunter/gathering peoples. Let us turn our attention to the first of the three societies.

The Hunter/Gatherers

Our ancestors, the hunter/gatherers, roamed our world forty thousand years ago. While there were many different types of lifestyles, there were also some common characteristics. Their life was a relatively simple unadorned routine. The males were basically the hunters who went in search of game and other prey. While the men were at the hunt, the women would be gathering roots, berries, and other fruits and vegetables that were available in the immediate vicinity. Such tasks for survival ensured aerobic exercise would be a part of daily life.

When the men returned, the group would feast. Their diet included much fresh fruit and vegetables, low-cholesterol meats (since the game of that period was much more lean), and few fats or sugars. There was no use of tobacco or alcohol.

Social life was simple and satisfying, if rudimentary by today's standards. There were small family units and the emphasis on responsibility to the larger group was very strong. It was a matter of survival against the elements, and every hand was needed. This sense of communality was enhanced by their religious rituals, as well as by meals, chores, and games enjoyed in common.

The hunter/gatherer society demonstrated reasonable mastery individually and as a group as members collaborated to ensure survival. Caring attachments were evidenced by their tribal life as noted above. The pace of time was essentially that of a nomadic wandering people. They followed the trails of the game and the fields of fruits and vegetables as biological need for survival dictated. They usually hunted/gathered for four days and then rested for three days. Life was hard, of course, and the leading causes of death were biological trauma, infectious disease, and childbirth complications (see Easton, Shostak, and Konner, 1988, for a more detailed presentation of these early peoples).

The lesson from history for us modern denizens of the same world was that this life-style with its mastery, attachments, exercise, sensible diet, and proper rest and pace of life was biologically attuned to the environment the hunter/gatherers lived in. The daily routine of this early culture and peoples allowed the body's natural processes in coping with stress to adapt most efficiently. The stress response, homeostasis, circadian rhythm, the general adaptation syndrome, and the assignment of meaning of these people led to good utilization of élan vital. There was the proper balance between the body's natural processes and a life-style that efficiently responded to its environment.

About twelve thousand years ago, the population began to increase and the relative availability of game decreased. These changes marked the first of the two fundamental shifts that we have spoken of. During this period, the hunter/gatherers became farmers. Virtually throughout the world, these wandering people settled into a life of agriculture and a less mobile life of small farming groups. From 10,000 BC even into our own century, survival became a matter of raising crops and, in time, raising herds of various animals.

The Agricultural/Farmers

The life-style of the agricultural/farming peoples began to shift in important ways. Hard exercise was still important for survival, but exercise was not uniformly required during the whole year. (There was less activity in the nongrowing seasons, for example.) Their diet changed also with the addition of grains, to be sure, but also, in addition to fruits and vegetables, there were increases in the consumption of sugars and meats saturated in high cholesterol fats. Tobacco and alcohol grew commonplace. Relaxation and rest periods in many ways became as seasonal as exercise had.

The agricultural/farming peoples, however, did retain reasonable mastery and a sense of caring attachments to others. Like the hunter/gatherers, survival for the farming peoples mandated the cooperation of everyone, and the blessings of nature. Concern for others and a belief in God were central to the lives of these men and women.

The emergence of agriculture was an important evolutionary shift in the human family's development. These changes created life stress: an imbalance between the way the body was built to cope with the world and the life-style and environment best suited to its most efficient functioning. Tens of thousands of years would now be required for the proper evolution and adaptation of our bodies to this new farming environment. During the course of these years, life stress would gradually lessen as the human family adapted to its new agricultural way of life.

A mere twelve thousand years later, generally from AD 1300 to AD 1600, an additional series of profound changes occurred. These changes, because they were so fundamentally different, have increased even further the process of adaptation to the environment that the human body must adjust to. Life stress has increased commensurately as well.

Since Daniel Boorstin (1978) has written of these changes at length, I will summarize the main points briefly. (1) Society began shifting from rural living in these small farming communities to life in large urban cities. In many ways the development of the United States was in part a result of the overflow of British subjects who moved to London. Bernard Bailyn (1986) has documented how these persons found European city life so overcrowded that they came to the New World and started their own cities in short order. (2) Society also moved from a period of simple rudimentary farming tools to an advanced machine-powered age. Today's industrial-age farmer is not shackled to his horse and hand-held hoe, but can utilize machinery, pesticides, computers, and advanced mete-orology to produce his goods. So far-reaching has been this shift that in the past few centuries a small number of our countrymen have produced enough food to feed all of us. For the first time in over forty-thousand years we are not all required to hunt or farm individually to survive, and these advances in technology have permeated all aspects of our society. We excel at mastery of our environment.

These first two basic changes have led to several additional changes. (3) Society is now moving from an existence of survival to one of leisure and affluence. Most of us take food, clothing, and shelter and medical care for granted. Yet, this has not been true for most of human history. We take material goods for granted. Yet, scarcity has been the more common norm. We take mobility for granted, and think nothing of going for a thirty-mile drive to visit friends. Yet, for most of human history, a large percentage of people never traveled further than ten miles from the place of their birth in their whole lives. The forty-hour work week, the summer vacation, these are the new kids on the block of history.

(4) Society is also moving, albeit slowly, from a period of subjugation for the average citizen to a period of equality. For most of human history, the average citizen was at the mercy of the king or the local landlord. In the past few centuries, great strides have been made in giving equal rights to everyone. This country was itself founded on the principle that all individuals are created equal. While equality is not yet fully true for women, blacks, and other minorities, civilization is moving in that direction. These shifts towards affluence and leisure and individual equality have led from a psychology of self-denial in an era of scarcity to a belief in self-realization. We are moving toward a period of emphasis on self-development and personal fulfillment.

Where will all of these changes take us as a society? No one knows the answer to that question. Many years of history and further development will need to pass before a clearer answer emerges. What we know now is this: all of the changes that were set in motion and noted by Boorstin have resulted at least initially in the development of the third society, the industrial/corporate peoples.

The Industrial/Corporate Peoples

Our third society dates traditionally from the Industrial Revolution at about AD 1850. It was at this time that energy was yoked to machinery. Water, steam, coal, oil, electricity, and then nuclear energy, each in turn was harnessed to machines to increase the production of goods. This society with which we are so familiar and take for granted is a very recent development in history, and quite different from the daily life of most of the human family in the history of recorded civilization. Because it is so different, we need to spend some time understanding the forces and values embedded in these routines on our journey toward becoming stress-resistant persons.

The Foundations of Industrial/Corporate Society. Philosophers are basically interested in the fundamental values and ways of perceiving and understanding the world around us. To the extent that a culture adheres to these philosophical positions, the power of such ideas becomes immense; and two philosophers have had such an impact on this third society.

Descartes spent long hours in an attempt to make sense of the world around us. Ultimately he felt the unifying principle for understanding was rational thought. His famous dictum, "I think, therefore I am," expresses clearly a firm belief in the power of reason as a resource for adaptive living. Hegel was the second philosopher to put forth a fundamental unifying principle. For him it was the inevitability of continuous change. For any given status quo (the thesis), there arises a new counterforce (the antithesis), which leads to a new resolution of the issue (the synthesis). For Hegel, events such as wars of revolution and the passing of human generations could be understood as processes of sequential change.

I believe that these two philosophical principles of rational thought and continuous change are rooted in most of the ways we relate to our environment and, as I will suggest, to each other. I say this because our culture, the industrial/corporate peoples, seem to value science and technology above all else, and rational thought and continuous change are the fundamental building blocks of science. If we were to choose three characteristics that would distinguish this third society from the hunter/gatherers and agricultural/farmers, it would be: science, the computer and material abundance.

Science is our understanding of the laws of nature, and our attempts to influence the processes that we have observed. The application of our understanding of the principles of math, physics, biology, and so forth to problems in our everyday life is known as technology. Both science and technology have been greatly influenced by rational thought and sequential change. Isaac Newton, who did much to develop the scientific method of inquiry, was fully committed to a rational understanding of the universe. He emphasized rational thought and believed the secrets and principles of nature resided within nature, and not in the eyes of the beholder. Unbiased observation would lead reason to unlock these secrets. Another well-known scientist, Albert Einstein, followed in the steps of Hegel. Einstein's theory of relativity has shown us that physical matter is in constant motion, much as Hegel had suggested decades earlier. The desk on which I write, which appears hard, sturdy, and firm, has been revealed by quantum physics to be in a form of constant motion. Rational thought and constant change are thus part of the bedrock of science, the foundation of much of our present culture.

Science, Technology, and Stress. The advances of science and technology have come to permeate all aspects of our daily lives, and have also contributed to the stress of life. From food production to shelter, clothing, and health care; from transportation to leisure activities, technology has minimized what was the daily struggle for existence. It has created an abundance of material affluence and choice. Without our fully being aware of it, the basic cultural values of rational thought and continuous change have become as common in our daily lives as the material goods we use. However, in addition to taking air conditioning and VCRs for granted, we have also come to assume that all change is good, and that reason can resolve all the problems that humans encounter. Neither assumption is always true.

One of the most far-reaching of our technological advances is the development of the computer, the symbol of both rational thought and rapid change. This mathematical, electronic machine that can compute faster than the human brain is at the leading edge of scientific advance. Large volumes of information can be processed, computed, analyzed, and evaluated for importance and priority in nanoseconds. The computer operates on nanoseconds that are one-billionth of a human second. It has been estimated that the world has changed more in the past fifty years than it did in the preceding five hundred years of human history. With the computer transferring millions of bits of information in nanoseconds, however, scientists predict the world will change even more quickly in the next twenty-five years than it has in the past fifty years. Indeed, computer scientists are now planning computers that will operate in picoseconds, one trillionth of a human second. This excessive rate of change creates stress for all of us. The technology already moves faster than human biology, and promises to move even faster in coming years.

Further, the computer's ability to transfer large bits of information and sums of money has facilitated the shift from small independent businessmen to huge multinational corporations. These large corporations are global, and have no allegiance to any particular nation or its peoples. Unlike you and me who have to sleep each day, multinational corporations are always open for business and making money each hour of each day. Consistent with good business practices, they manufacture where the costs of raw products and labor are cheapest, and sell where prices are apt to be highest. The system has evolved to the point where a small number of men and women have a powerful voice in the economic affairs of the millions of people in the world, and the person without such a voice usually has less mastery and increased stress.

Through their acquisitions, corporations often own or control the natural resources, the manufacturing processes, the transportation service to the markets, and, often, the retail stores themselves. This concentration of resources has led, for the first time in human history, to a culture of great affluence, wealth, and a plurality of choices concerning material goods. These are not insignificant gains. However, as with any form of concentrated power, such power can breed unwanted excesses and stress for others. The corporation that brought about this change is, and will remain, a permanent institution in our culture much as the church and the universities were in the Middle Ages. We must adjust to the life change it creates even as we monitor its impact on our lives.

How have such material advances affected us humans? A well-known sociologist, Auguste Comte, surveyed the extensive human misery about him in the 1850s, and sounded a hopeful note for mankind. It was he who proposed harnessing the newly emerging advances in science and technology and applying this positive knowledge to meet the human needs of people, to brighten the lives of the average citizen. A century later, with the advances in housing, nutrition, sanitation, national self-defense, transportation, and business, as we have just seen, Comte would and should be justly satisfied with his sociological forethought. Science has improved the material well-being of many people.

The Corporate Peoples and Stress. What are the lives of these people of the third society like? How have science, the computer, and material affluence affected human life?

Unlike the previous two societies (the hunter/gatherers and agricultural/farmers), the industrial/corporate peoples have made huge strides in mastery of the environment. We reshape the physical environment to conform to our psychological needs and wants. If we tire of one environment, we jet away to another. Where people had to work hard just to survive, we now have leisure time for self-realization and personal development. We drive ourselves, however, relentlessly for personal achievement and the acquisition of material goods, and increase our life stress in doing so. We want to have it all.

There have been other changes too. Even with an awareness of good health practices, our diets now include less fruits and vegetables and more saturated fats. (Since these fats in animals are where cancer-causing pesticides and growth hormones are stored, eating such fats leads to their storage in our bodies also.) There is more use of alcohol and tobacco, and in general (except for a relatively small segment of the population) much less exercise because our technological advances like cars, TVs, and so forth make us sedentary. As our sedentary life-style increases, so does our general body weight. For example, Yankee Stadium was built in the 1920s. When it was renovated in the 1970s, there was room for eight thousand less seats because the new seats had to be wider for the hips of us affluent people. Lastly, we rarely relax because there is so much to do, so many new things to acquire, so many choices to be made. As our material well-being in this life has increased, our interest in the next life has declined in equal proportions. All of these various changes tax the body's capacity to cope effectively, and increase our life stress.

Changes in types of disease have occurred also. While life has eased considerably from the hunter/gatherers society, disease in the second and third societies has not only remained a part of life, but has increased considerably in both type and quantity. Included on the list are: atherosclerosis, hypertension, stroke, heart disease, cancer, diabetes, cirrhosis of the liver, lung disease, emphysema, even hemorrhoids and dental caries. Seventy-five percent of us now die from these diseases of industrial civilization. As industrialization proceeds, the virulence of these illnesses grows also. Heart disease, for example, the leading cause of death in our own time, was not even on the list of the ten leading causes of death in AD 1900. Our farming and industrial progress appears to be taxing the body and the environment it inhabits.

Technology and Human Conduct

Behavioral Changes. Now that we have had a chance to consider the forces shaping our own times, let us return to the driver behavior at traffic lights that we discussed earlier in the chapter. You will remember that the car permits personal achievement and the acquisition of goods in relative isolation from other persons, even though other persons may be important resources in reducing stress by helping us solve problems and regulating our health.

What did we see at the traffic lights, and is it in any way related to our culture's major forces: science and technology, the computer, and material acquisitions? The last is fairly clear. When we observed such driver behavior, we found people with material goods: goods for personal grooming, goods for nourishment, goods for getting work done, goods for "leisure" time. There is no doubt that the quality of physical life has improved because of science and technology, and the material goods they have yielded. Material goods are everywhere; however, what traffic light behavior suggests is that there are too many goods to use in the time that we have to use them. We have to do several things at once to participate in everything, to attain what is considered acceptable personal achievement.

What else are we able to observe? Frantic behavior, surely. Here are drivers using sixty seconds of time to try to catch up. The computer that drives science and technology, and general production of goods and services may move at nanosecond speeds, but traffic behavior suggests that humans cannot. There is too much to do too quickly in too little time. Human endurance cannot keep up with the computer pace. Computer speed alters daily human life, and the body's natural processes to cope by moving faster than humans can. Homeostasis, circadian rhythms, the general adaptation syndrome, and the like are not only not given tens of thousands of years to evolve, but are required to adapt to rates of change a billion times faster than the human biological time of which they are a part.

We see the fallout from this individual frustration, this sense of powerlessness in the face of the rat race at the traffic lights. Not only are we cut off from people, humans who could buffer the impact of stress, but we abuse the very people who could be so helpful by rude driving patterns, obscene gestures, and the like. I really don't believe that people set out in the morning to behave this way toward others, but the cultural pace for success often results in this unfortunate outcome. Equally important is the abuse of self. The anger that keeps the physiology of stress on unnecessarily, and the use of drugs and alcohol to medicate that personal distress, are signs of demoralization, anxiety, depression, and illness.

Traffic light behavior seems to suggest that none of us can have it all, that we pay a price in physical and mental well-being whenever we try to have it all.

Extreme Personality Types. Moreover, there has emerged in our current era two personality styles that push personal achievement and material acquisition to ever further extremes. One of these personality styles you have already met at the beginning of the chapter.

Type A's. Mr. Wallace, our driven man in the intensive care unit, personifies what is called the Type A Behavior Pattern (TABP). While there are problems assessing TABP, and at times, conflicting findings, individuals with this style of coping generally behave exactly as Mr. Wallace does. Hardworking, time-urgent, managing several tasks at once, intensely competitive, never relaxing, bereft of true friends, and very hostile. (Type B behavior pattern is the reverse of this: easygoing, reasonably paced, less competitive, and so forth.)

Type A's populate our daily routines. We all know of some Type A persons. What you may not know is that for all their frantic activity, they not only don't accomplish more, their diverted attention span leads easily to errors, and their hostility leads their co-workers to withdraw from them. Type A behavior costs companies money.

Of the components of Type A behavior listed above, present research findings suggest that hostility appears to be the singularly most dangerous marker. Its presence indicates a highly stressed person, and, just as Type A's have the behavior of Mr. Wallace, so they also have his disease. Premature heart disease and premature death are frequently found in these persons. They often boast that they don't get ulcers, they give them. This may be true, but it is also true that they often get heart disease.

Narcissists. Our second cultural personality style is also focused on material goods and is bereft of caring attachments. These individuals glory in their own self-aggrandizement. They are entitled, self-centered, and selfish. They are called narcissists, after the figure in mythology (Narcissus) who was so intent on examining his "self" in a reflecting pool that he fell in and drowned.

Narcissists always seek adulation, and present themselves and their goods as arrogantly better than the rest of us. In my counseling experience, this behavior that is so odious to others actually masks a deeply rooted sense of self-hate. Usually in their childhood years, narcissists were given many material goods by parents and other adult family members who spent little personal time with these individuals. In the course of growing up, and being given things rather than the presence of people, the child felt that there must be some reason people were avoiding his or her presence. Children often blame themselves and state to themselves that they are the cause of the problem. It is the child who is defective. The seeds of self-hatred are sown as is this process of self-blame. Unfortunately, in adulthood such seeds yield a full harvest of self-denigration. Psychologically, this process is so painful that the human mind so afflicted seeks relief by behavior in just the opposite way— a public presentation of self-importance to gain some psychic relief from the self-hate. The next time you are treated rudely by an arrogant person, you'll be able to cope with your own stress by remembering the basic process of self-hatred that is really the root of such behavior. The self-hate and arrogance in the narcissist creates continuous life stress because other persons avoid them. (If you wish to read further, Christopher Lasch, 1978, has written an interesting book on this topic.)

Lessons From History

Do science and technology meet all of the human needs of the industrial/corporate peoples as Auguste Comte suggested? As we have noted, technology has yielded vast improvements in the quality of our physical well-being; there can be no doubt about that. But does technology meet all our human needs? I think not. Like most everything else in life, technology has its downside, and table 1 illustrates some of the central problems.

First, you will recall that the human organism needs tens of thousands of years to adjust to major shifts. Table 1 presents the three major societies with the agricultural/farmers and industrial/corporate cultures being two major shifts. Since tens of thousands of years have not passed, it should not surprise us that we feel the stress of life. There is immense change occurring in the most basic fabric in our culture, change occurring faster than we can keep pace with.

Table 1

Daily Life—A Comparison of Three Societies:

Factors	Hunter/ Gatherers	Agricultural/ Farmers	Industrial/ Corporate
Reasonable Mastery	Yes	Yes	No (Excessive)
Commitment	Yes	Yes	Limited
Life-style			
Sensible Diet	Yes	No	No
Hard Exercise	Yes	Yes (Seasonal)	No
Relaxation	Yes	Yes (Seasonal)	No
Attachments to Others	Yes	Yes	Limited
Time:	Biological Need	The Seasons	Nanoseconds

Second, you will remember that our natural bodily processes for coping with stress evolved to work most efficiently in a hunter/ gatherer environment. Another quick inspection of table 1 will suggest just how far we are removed from adaptive body response in our industrial/corporate age. We engage in excessive mastery, and deviate extensively from the optimal body/environment balance that was fixed tens of thousands of years ago. Our sense of mastery, commitment, life-style, and utilization of time are all putting us on the fast track to life stress. Some of these shifts started in the agricultural/farmers period, but they have accelerated greatly in our time.

The third important lesson from the table is the relative absence of caring attachments among industrial peoples. As Albee (1980) has pointed out to us, and we have seen in chapter 2, caring attachments are crucial to a relatively stress-free life. Yet, in our culture some have overemphasized mastery and material goods (Type A's, for example), others avoid caring attachments (narcissists, for example), and we have seen similar patterns of disregarding others in our own behavior at traffic lights.

A reasonable question at this point is this: Do we really need caring attachments in this day and age? The divorce rate is about 50 percent, yet these divorced men and women seem to go on. Survival is not a daily and literally life-threatening situation. Possibly we can de-emphasize our attachments to and our need for others. Maybe stress-resistant people are wrong on this point.

The medical research is compelling, and demonstrates that we have not outgrown our need for caring attachments to others. Dr. Leonard Sagan (1987) recently studied the health of many nations, including our own. He found that most industrial countries had their best levels of health from AD 1900–1955. Improvements in sanitation, nutrition, public health, and medical care do not explain this phenomenon. Instead, Dr. Sagan found family life to be the key. Human attachment between parents and children accounted for this dramatic improvement.

During the first fifty years of this century, as daily survival

Technology Can Be Mind Numbing.

"I thought you might be looking for this. The garage door has been going up and down for the past ten minutes."

became less of an immediate issue, adults had time to devote to each other and to their children. Parents had time to prepare their children to function in society and to provide the emotional support necessary for growth in these formative years. Society had a reasonable balance between mastery and attachment.

After 1955, as the race for personal achievement and material goods accelerated, our human attachments became casualties. As divorce, single parenting, teenage parenting, mobility, infidelity, and homelessness increased, our health decreased. Even in an age of advanced medical science, our health as a nation is declining even for women who have long seemed to have some form of resistance to early death. The medical evidence seems generally clear and consistent: none of us can have it all.

Is it possible in this industrial/corporate day and age to lead a reasonably contented life, free of undue ill health? The answer from stress-resistant persons is yes. We can see more clearly now how they have blended the best life-style choices of the hunter/gatherer period with the advances of a technological age. They have found a helpful balance between reasonable mastery and caring attachments in today's world. They have good health and a sense of well-being. They realize that without such a balance, stressful life events will increase the potential for demoralization and illness.

5

ILLNESS: THE PERIL OF IGNORING STRESS

The tragedy of life is what dies inside a man while he lives.
—Albert Schweitzer

We have met the enemy and he is us.
—Pogo

Damn it, she thought, who has time for this? The stabbing pain in her abdomen was back, and at twelve noon no less. Usually this associate of hers was a late-afternoon phenomenon. It made her angry. She experienced this pain in her gut as a personal affront to her efficiency. After all she had just gotten over the flu. She sat at her desk, made her phone calls, and tried to ignore the pain. Maybe she needed a drink.

Eileen was a go-getter, and she had just landed her firm, Moss and Hart Advertising, their largest account ever. She would have to travel more and be away from Josh for longer periods of time, but promotion was in the air. According to the latest trend-setting magazines, she was a prototype of the New Age woman. And up-and-coming career on Lexington Avenue in New York City. Expense-account dinners. Courtesy limosines.

She also had a mortgage she couldn't afford, an hour-and-a-half commute each way to work, long hours at her desk, and Joshua. As a single parent, she worried a good deal about Joshua. The divorce had been terrible for both of them. He had cried for weeks. He was seven now, and needed his father more than one weekend a month. She felt guilty when she wasn't with him, guilty about his twelve hour days in day care, but it was his loneliness that pained her most. What kind of life was this for a kid?

What kind of life was this for his mother? Too much to do, no personal time, no social life, no fun. She and Josh deserved better than this. God knows, she worked hard enough. She doubled over in pain. She reached for the phone. That drink of hers would be a double.

As we have noted, stress-resistant persons are diligent in minimizing or avoiding the painful predicaments Eileen now finds herself in. They know, better than many of us, the distress that can result from not managing stress wisely.

What prevents most of us from understanding the really harmful consequences that stress can lead to is the fact that such outcomes are most often not immediate. Unlike a bad bruise or broken bone, it often takes many years before a stress-related medical problem becomes disabling. It can also be many years before heart disease manifests itself. It takes several years for emphysema and/or lung cancer to occur in the smoker. Stress-resistant persons start early on in life to avoid such negative outcomes. They realize that modern medicine can successfully treat trauma, infectious disease, and childbirth complications, the banes of the hunter/gatherers. They also realize that the remaining diseases are a function of industrial society and need to be avoided. Effective copers plan ahead.

We can do likewise. The present material contains a representative sample of some of the major physical and mental illnesses that may be stress-related. Eileen, whom we just met, had three: the flu, irritable-bowel syndrome (her stomach pain), and alcoholism. The lesson in each is clear. Unmanaged stress can have painful, even lethal, consequences for all of us. By understanding the causes of these diseases, we can map out strategies to minimize their occurrence in our own lives. Planning now will augment our own stress resistance and increase the quality of our lives in the future.

When Anxiety Is Not Stress-Related

Let us begin first with the diseases that are *not* primarily stress-related, even though the illness may feel like too much life stress. Some physical and psychiatric diseases have symptoms similar to anxiety and stress: racing heart, trembling limbs, perspiration, feelings of fear, anxiety, and panic.

Certain medical diseases that have little to do with stress can cause symptoms such as those just listed. Hypoglycemia, (low blood sugar), Addison's disease (adrenal insufficiency), an overactive thyroid gland, temporal lobe epilepsy, mitral valve prolapse, inner ear disturbances, and the aftereffects of concussion are such medical diseases of the body. Additionally, the excessive use of amphetamines (including diet pills), and withdrawal from alcohol or sedatives can also appear with symptoms similar to those of stress.

Some medical diseases primarily affect the brain rather than the body. Again, one should not assume the symptoms are due only to stress. Agoraphobia (the fear of going outside alone), panic attacks, and severe depressions that can leave the patient extremely agitated and restless are all examples of such biological diseases, just as arthritis and diabetes are biological diseases. The anxiety-like symptoms in these illnesses are usually not primarily associated with stress. Even though life stress may at times aggravate these medical problems, they are medical diseases.

There are clear ways to diagnose these medical problems, and there are sound treatments to resolve these ills. *Strategies for becoming stress-resistant will not solve these problems.* Good programs for coping with stress should begin with a physical exam to rule out any medical problems that may appear to be due to. stress. Such an exam will also help you assess your capacity for an aerobic exercise program. See your physician first. If you also have any of these stress-related symptoms frequently, bring these to the attention of your doctor for proper evaluation. Bring them to your physician's attention even if you believe them to be solely stress-related.

The General Impact of Stress-Related Illness

True stress-related diseases do take their toll. Drs. Edward Charlesworth and Ronald Nathan (1984) have recently reported that over thirty million Americans have some form of heart or blood vessel disease, one million have heart attacks each year, twenty-five million suffer from high blood pressure, eight million have ulcers, and twelve million are alcoholics. Nineteen billion dollars were lost by businesses in the United States because of

premature employee death, fifteen billion dollars because of alcoholism, and another fifteen billion dollars from other stress related
absenteeism. These are big league statistics, and we should all
consider them thoughtfully. Stress-related diseases weaken us as
individuals, as families, as communities, and as a nation.

The effects of stress do not impact on all of us with the same
intensity. There are known differences in geographical locations,
career choice, and gender.

Research has shown that it has been generally more stressful to
live in the Western and Southern parts of the United States. Daily
life in some states in the Union has also been shown to be more
stressful. The most recent research data indicated that Alabama
was the most stressful, and Iowa, the least stressful when the level
of stress was measured by fifteen factors including the number of
business failures, workers on strike, unemployment claims filed,
divorces, infant deaths, and mortgage foreclosures. Such findings
demonstrate how the environment, including even our geographical location, can influence our level of stress.

Secondly, we know that certain occupations place the individual
in that job at higher risk for stress-related diseases. Physicians,
psychologists, critical care nurses, dentists, air traffic controllers,
and news reporters appear to be more burdened by work-site stress
than judges, lawyers, and public officials. The reasons for this are
unclear. One possible link for the high-risk group is that their work
requires them to respond often to immediate crises in people's lives.
This continuous source of stress may account for the increased
stress related problems over the course of the individual's career.

Thirdly, it is clear that men have been at much higher risk for
stress-related diseases and premature death than females (Statistical
Abstracts of the U.S., 1984). To begin with there are more male
infant deaths than female infant deaths. As they grow older, males
have been twice as likely to die from heart disease than females,
three times more likely than females to die from pneumonia,
influenza, accidents, and adverse drug effects, and three times more
likely than females to commit suicide.

Males also seem to die more on Saturdays than on other days of
the week. No one really knows why, as yet, but the researchers
speculate that out-of-condition males who are sedentary all week
decide to become very active on the weekends (e.g., chopping

firewood). Such activity is assumed to overtax the heart muscle which responds by stopping. If you are a male employee and your female colleague wishes you a nice weekend on Friday afternoon, remember that it is easy for her to say, but harder for you to comply.

While all of this would appear to be good news for women, research in the mid-1970s (Barnett, Biener, and Baruch, 1987) began to document what appears to be generally declining health for women. In some studies women were dying earlier than the men. These are early reports and will bear careful watching. It may be that as women become highly competitive in the work place, increase their smoking, and the like, they may be surrendering their heretofore greater resiliency in responding to life stress. It remains unclear.

Underlying the majority of these statistics is a common culprit, a fundamental life-stress for all of us. Economic instability, as we have noted, is the single, most pervasive, continuous source of stress in our society. Lack of adequate finances has been related to every stress-related illness from increased infant mortality to tooth decay.

Dr. M. Harvey Brenner (1973) has provided us with some statistics. He noted that a 1.49 percent increase in unemployment in 1970 was followed in the subsequent five years by a 2.79 percent increase in deaths due to alcoholism and heart disease, by a 4.7 percent increase in admissions to mental hospitals, and by an increase in the suicide rate to 5.7 percent. Such findings of this type are continuously being reported. Not enough money leads to an increase in stress-related diseases.

All of us need the basic essentials to stay alive, and all of us would agree that having enough money to enjoy life is a preferable state of affairs. Unless you are born or marry into established wealth, however, none of us can make enough money in one working lifetime to have it all. Here again we can observe that excessive emphasis on the acquisition of money and material goods places us at increased risk for stress-related illnesses.

Untreated Life Stress and Medical Disease

We begin our survey of the potential consequences of untreated life stress by focusing on the nation's leading cause of death.

Heart Disease. There are many different types of heart disease, and the development of each type is equally complicated. Some general facts are known, however, about the possible relationships between life stress, life-style choices, and heart disease.

Sudden overwhelming stressful life events can seemingly increase the risk for heart disease and premature death in apparently healthy people. We saw some examples of this in Doctor Engle's research (1971) in chapter 2, where sudden loss of loved ones led to death. Such perceived stress appears to disrupt the homeostatic balance and rhythmic pace of the heart. Such disruptions can cause the heart to misfire and stop.

Life-style choices also appear to influence the onset and progression of various types of heart disease that occur over the course of longer periods of time. Heart disease appears to be a multiple risk illness, and certain of the markers for increased risk of heart dysfunction and disease are known to the medical community. As we have noted, these include age, being male, high levels of cholesterol, hypertension, heavy cigarette smoking, diabetes mellitus, a parental history of heart disease, obesity, physical inactivity, and abnormalities of an electrocardiogram.

An examination of these markers will show some of them to be under our control. Any of us could exercise reasonable mastery by adhering to a diet low in the saturated fats that can lead to higher serum cholesterol, by not smoking, by maintaining good body weight, and by exercising and being physically active.

The absence of caring attachments may also be another possible risk factor for heart disease. Less attention has been paid to this possibility, but the research has shown that individuals who remain socially isolated and/or cut off from caring attachments have been found to have greater risk for heart disease. The absence of caring attachments may be one of the contributing factors. We noted in chapter 2 the work of Drs. Engle, Weisman, and Hackett demonstrated sudden cardiac death upon the loss of an important attachment. "Anniversary death" also illustrates this sudden death phenomenon. An anniversary death is the sudden death in an otherwise usually healthy person on the anniversary of the loss of someone or something that was important to the individual. For example, Richard Nixon was reelected President on January 20, 1973. He announced his intention to dismantle the Great Society on January 21, 1973. Former President Lyndon Johnson, the author of the Great Society, died from a sudden heart attack on January 22, 1973. Is this just concidence? History is full of similar examples. Many of us have also known couples very close in life. One dies, the other dies within hours or days.

A chronic absence of caring attachments also appears to be a possible source of life stress that may result in continuous wear and tear with a similar increased risk for heart disease. Henry Abbott Wallace, whom we met earlier in the Intensive Care Unit, and, to some extent, Eileen in this chapter's example, are prototypic candidates for chronic heart disease. Each is a Type A behavior person with the sense of time urgency, excessive work, and hostility that we have previously noted. The TABP person's preoccupation with excessive mastery leaves limited time, if any, for caring attachments. The absence of such attachments may place such persons at increased risk.

Stress resistant persons with their emphasis on reasonable mastery and caring attachments thus minimize the risk of heart disease. We can do likewise.

Cancer. The causes of cancer remain unclear. It appears to be a disease of aging whose probability of occurrence is increased by excessive exposure to environmental toxins. There also seems to be a genetic predisposition in some cases.

Stress and cancer do not appear to be directly related. However, to the extent that individuals use cigarettes or alcohol in their lifestyles and/or to cope with life stress, the possibilities of contracting certain types of cancer increase.

Smoking. Repeated medical evidence demonstrates convincingly that cigarette smoking is a major cause of lung cancer. The cells of the lung lose their capacity for elasticity and are destroyed. The cancers associated with smoking can also impair the liver, stomach, and heart of the victims. For far too many, death ensues.

Alcohol. We shall look at the range of health problems caused by alcohol abuse in its own right later in the chapter. We need to note here, however, that alcohol abuse is also associated with increased cancer risk. The abuse of alcohol has been associated with cancers of the mouth, tongue, larynx, and esophagus.

Heart disease and cancer are obviously complicated medical diseases. However, there is increasing evidence that untreated life stress may be a factor in the onset of some such illnesses. The same appears to be true for mental distress.

Untreated Life Stress and Mental Distress

When we are frustrated by too many problems, and are feeling overwhelmed in our ability to cope, many of us may turn that frustration on others or on ourselves in less than adequate ways of coping. Here are some of the more common (and ineffective) strategies:

Harm to Others. When people are frustrated and angry, they often lash out at others who are not a part of the problem. A common example is that when our boss gets angry with us, we feel powerless to attack him or her, and so we scream at our spouse, or children, or pet. Some people even throw books at the wall. While some psychologists continue to debate whether it is better to keep your anger in or let it out, the real key lies in getting the problem solved (Tavris, 1982). The angry individual must address the issue or person that is making him or her feel helpless and frustrated. Yelling at a third party will not solve the problem. It only serves to shatter the self-confidence and self-esteem of all who are involved in this displaced anger.

Physically or sexually abusing others is equally unacceptable. While such abuse may be a last desperate act to maintain control or to sustain human attachment when all other attempts have failed (van der Kolk, 1987), it is an unacceptable, ineffective, and repugnant way to deal with life stress. The physical abuse of one's spouse (male or female), of one's children, of one's elderly parents in nursing homes, and of one's neighbors have all been shown to increase when the perpetrator is under stress. The sexual abuse of one's children and the rapes of other adults have likewise been shown to increase during times of stress. Twenty-five to thirty percent of all women have been sexually abused by some male they knew; one in five males have also been sexually abused by a male or female. Often such perpetrators commit this crime when they are faced with life stress.

Homicide, street crime, and motor vehicle accidents all increase when angry people under stress lash out at the wrong person. In

1988 alone, half of all the traffic fatalities, twenty-five thousand deaths, were alcohol related. These drivers were by definition not coping with life stress before they got behind the wheel. Such drivers take a human life every twenty-two minutes.

The havoc wreaked on the victims of these various tragedies is pervasive, crippling, and of lifelong duration, if left untreated. Children and adults silently carry the scars of such violence. The victim may never trust anyone again, the victim may be afraid to be intimate, the victim may have recurring intrusive thoughts of the event, the victim may be chronically tense or have a continuing sleep disorder, the victim may have lifelong feelings of poor self-esteem. We have a term for these outcomes in medicine: it is called Posttraumatic Stress Disorder (PTSD). It is the same affliction often experienced by many veterans of war. While many effective treatments for PTSD exist, the tragedy of the initial violence is further compounded by the all-too-common false assumption of victims that, because the event happened to them, they are somehow to blame, they are somehow defective, and not worthy of treatment. Thus, the available treatments are not sought out by the victim and may not be known of by family and friends. The scars are then carried to the grave.

Violence to others or to property is never a solution to managing stress.

Harm to Self. Many people under stress are equally as harsh on themselves. Such individuals may do harmful things to themselves when confronted with life stress. They may behave ineffectively, develop psychosomatic disease, abuse substances, or take their own lives.

Problematic Behavior. People under stress often eat, drink, or smoke too much; they run traffic lights, and in so doing put themselves and others in potentially lethal situations. They allow their marriages to end in divorce; they go in search of affairs that only increase their stress. We have all observed examples of such self-defeating patterns of behavior.

Psychosomatic Disease. In addition to these problematic behaviors, some persons develop psychosomatic diseases. In such illnesses, the psychological stress in the mind results in physical disease in the body. As we have noted, about seventy-five percent of all the aches and pains we take to our physicians are thought to be psychosomatic. Disease states such as asthma, headache,* psoriasis, spastic colon, and ulcer are all examples of possible psychosomatic disorders. While individuals may have a certain biological predisposition to develop one type of psychosomatic disease or another, they remain in good health if they manage their life stress well. If they cope poorly, the psychosomatic diseases flare up.

Suicide. In addition to problematic behavior and psychosomatic disease, other persons use a third strategy that harms the self. They take their own lives by committing suicide. Sometimes people attempt to harm themselves to communicate to us that they are overwhelmed by the life stress that they are encountering. Such gestures are cries for help. At other times, some individuals feel so overwhelmed and hopeless about the future that they end their own lives. They have gone beyond the point of gesturing. In our country, for example, one teenager commits suicide every fifty-nine minutes, often because he or she feels overwhelmed by life stress.

The rate of suicide in our country has always been fairly constant each year since records were kept from about the time of the Civil War. This kind of yearly consistency has suggested to some medical researchers that suicide might have a biological basis, and recent evidence from Scandinavia (Justice, 1988) suggests that this view may be accurate. It appears that some people may be born with a lower threshold for tolerating life's problems, and thus become intensely depressed under stress. A sense of hopelessness, a lack of mastery skills, and this lowered biological threshold may contribute to the suicide. While further research needs to be done, these findings suggest that the surviving loved ones of the suicide victim should not berate themselves for not having prevented the lethal act. Suicide may be, in part, a medical disease.

Alcohol Abuse. The remaining two forms of self-harm are alcohol and drug related. People often turn to drugs when they are feeling overwhelmed by stress. Have you ever thought of yourself as

---

*While most Americans consider headache to be stress-related, this is not always so. Some types of headache are not primarily stress-related. You may have a nonstress type of headache, such as cluster headache, or possibly an allergy to pollens, certain foods, or chemicals. Headache can also be due to more serious medical illnesses such as aneurysms, intracranial bleeding, and tumors. If you have recurring headaches you should see your physician.

a moving target? As one of the clay pigeons at target practice? If you have ever been in a motor vehicle in the very early hours of a Sunday morning, you have been such a target. You were a target because every tenth driver coming at you at 55 mph. is so intoxicated that he or she is physically unable to operate his or her vehicle. In the hands of a drunken driver, a two-thousand-pound vehicle becomes a lethal weapon for the driver and everyone around that driver.

The stress-resistant persons in my research minimize the use of alcohol with good reason. Too much alcohol inhibits the body's coordination of movement. It disrupts the transmission of information from the senses to the brain; it impairs higher brain functions like thinking and problem solving; and it can anesthetize memory so that the individual cannot remember what happened when he or she awakes the next morning. (This last process is called a blackout.) Such disruptions of body chemistry compromise any attempts we may make to resolve life stress, and they certainly make it impossible to drive a motor vehicle.

People start drinking for many reasons. Sometimes the drinking and subsequent abuse is genetic: the body craves alcohol. Some people may drink because they are hypoglycemic and crave the sugar in alcohol. Others drink because they are depressed. Still others use alcohol to self-medicate a variety of diseases that they have not brought to their physician's attention. Many drink to have fun, or to be part of the group. The late Norman Zinberg, MD, o Harvard Medical School, has shown us that many persons develop an alcohol addiction with enough alcohol ingestio this way, all of the reasons cited above may result in alcoho

Each of these persons may become addicted to alcohol speaking of skid-row alcoholics, I am speaking of men in all social classes just like you and me. Many wo children, own their homes, and are responsive needs. Their functioning at each of these tasks, l impaired because of their alcohol abuse. On addicted to alcohol; two in ten teenagers ar They are human beings like you and m serious medical disease.

This medical disease has far-reach abuse is linked to brain injuries, he we have noted, cirrhosis of the liver, infants, and very serious depression. (We frequently see patients in the clinics who are drinking heavily but are complaining of depression. They do not realize the depression is a side effect of alcohol itself.) Clearly, this is a disease and an ineffective coping strategy to be avoided.

How would anyone know if he or she were an alcoholic? This is a good question, and there is a concise answer. If your drinking is getting you into trouble, you are an alcoholic.

Your boss may tell you to sober up, your spouse may threaten to leave, your children may be estranged from you, you may have been arrested for drunken driving, you may feel sick. In any of these examples, the person is in trouble because of alcohol. This definition makes no reference to sex, age, body weight, or type of alcoholic beverage involved. Any trouble related to alcohol is alcohol abuse.

Here are four questions we use in our clinics: (1) Do you need an eye-opener? (2) Do you get angry when people discuss alcohol? (3) Has anyone told you to cut back on your consumption? (4) Do you feel guilty? If you answer yes to two or more of these statements you have a problem with alcohol. Helpful treatments are available. There are better strategies for managing stress.

Substance Abuse. Like alcohol, the abuse of street drugs and some prescription medicines leads to psychological and physical addiction. These drugs impair our capacity to cope with life stress, and have serious consequences for the abuser and his or her loved ones.

Many people appear to use drugs to treat their discomfort in the face of life stress. One of my colleagues here at Harvard Medical School, Edward Khantzian, MD (1985) has developed what he refers to as the self-medication hypothesis. It is his belief that individuals use certain types of drugs to medicate different types of painful feeling states associated with the stress of life. I have grouped his findings in table 1. Amphetamines (including diet pills, cocaine, and crack) are used to relieve depressions. Alcohol and barbiturates (including sleeping pills) are primarily used to relieve anxiety. Opiates seem to be used to relieve anger and rage in people. Doctor Blair Justice (1988) suggests that in some persons self-medication of feelings may also have a biological basis. More research will be needed to help us sort out these matters.

I would like to extend Drs. Khantzian's and Justice's work one

Table 1

Substance Abuse and the Self-Medication Hypothesis:

Substance	Type of Psychological Distress
Amphetamines Cocaine }	Depression
Alcohol Barbiturates }	Anxiety
Opiates }	Anger

step further. It is my belief that these various painful feelings may have another possible basis in some. I believe that many alcoholics and substance abusers may also be self-medicating the feelings that arise from the lack of caring human attachments. Excessive emphasis on personal striving and material goods leaves us little time for others. This painful state hurts, and some may self-medicate this loneliness with substances. Such substance abuse is essentially not found in stress-resistant people.

As with alcohol, substance abuse alters normal body and brain chemistry, may cause dependency, and prevents the learning of better solutions to the stressful problem.

As with alcohol, helpful treatments are available. There are better strategies for managing stress and in the second half of this book we shall look in more detail at some of these more effective strategies.

Part 2

STRATEGIES FOR BECOMING STRESS-RESISTANT: COMMON ISSUES

6

MASTERY: YOUR LIFE-STYLE AND PROJECT *SMART*

*The only way to keep your health is to
. . . do what you'd rather not.*
—Mark Twain

*Whenever I get the urge to exercise,
I lie down until it goes away.*
—James Thurber

The doors of the moving van slammed shut. They had to be out by today. He lit a cigarette, finished off his now cold coffee, and parked his potbelly on the hood of his Buick. Not bad, he thought. At five feet eight inches and two hundred sixty pounds, he was not your typical giant among men, but Robert Farnum was the new vice-president for sales. Final destination: world corporate headquarters, Minnesota.

It hadn't been easy for the Farnum family. Nine moves in as many years had been unsettling for Sheila and the kids. Nine different pediatricians. Nine different school systems. Nine different dry cleaners. He knew they were all overwhelmed. They rarely had meals together, the kids were depressed, he never got to the health club, and Sheila had taken to staying at home.

He also knew she was drinking. It had been embarrassing when it had first come up. He and Sheila had been called to school when their fourteen-year-old son had been found selling marijuana to a fifth grader. In anger, the boy had told the school authorities that his mother did drugs too. But that was last year's school system, and Robert hoped it would all go away. Still, he thought about it often when his recurring insomnia kept him up most of the night.

The family had pleaded with him to stay put. He and Sheila had

had a huge argument over this, and his eight-year-old daughter had stayed in her room for three days and three nights. He would have none of it. They would move. No desert nomads, this family. They were the new corporate migrants on the road to the good life. Chasing after time for a space to live.

The Farnums are walking statistics, serious health problems waiting to happen. Robert's career aspirations with its dependence on mobility has monopolized his family's time. Their basic life-style, which could have the potential to mitigate their stress, is so far removed from the healthy ways of the hunter/gatherer peoples as to become a source of stress in its own right.

Bob and his family are not alone in their forgetfulness of what could be helpful. In the Surgeon General's Report of 1988, two-thirds of the deaths in the United States appeared attributable to poor dietary habits (deaths due to coronary heart disease, stroke, atherosclerosis, diabetes, and some cancers). Alcohol abuse was associated with many others (cirrhosis of the liver, accidents, suicide).

These are things that we can have control over, and we shall explore how to gain such reasonable mastery. We will focus first on seven basic life-style choices that we can employ to enhance our sense of reasonable mastery over our lives. Next, we'll look briefly at how time constraints and recurring mobility can complicate these helpful ways of coping. Then, I will outline Project SMART, the basic approach that I have developed to help in getting started toward these sensible life-style choices, even in a fast-paced era of nanoseconds.

Reasonable Mastery: Your Weekly Routine

People are not machines and we cannot push ourselves re-lentlessly without its taking a toll on our health and well-being. Drs. Nedra Belloc and Lester Breslow (1972) have identified a series of life-style choices that are known to improve one's sense of health and well-being. These choices can be gradually introduced into our daily routines over a period of several months. Since these seven factors are known ways to increase stress-resistance, it is in our own best interest to implement them in our own lives in small and manageable steps.

No Smoking (#1). Since 1982, the surgeons general of the United States have been continuously warning us of the health hazards of cigarette smoking. It is hard to dispute such consistent findings.

Smoking has several harmful side effects. It increases your blood pressure and heart rate. It increases your metabolism, that part of your body that burns energy. In this way, your body is always in overdrive. Smoking lowers high density lipoproteins, and increases carbon monoxide in the blood. Smoking is also a nicotine addiction and its presence in the body as a foreign substance increases life stress. A smoker stuck in traffic has two life-stress problems: smoking plus the traffic. Two problems: twice as much élan vital is required.

The toll from smoking on health and well-being is high. Smoking significantly increases the chances of getting lung cancer and heart disease. Recent research has also demonstrated that your nonsmoking loved ones are at greater disease risk from passively breathing your smoke.

Smoking kills because it destroys the body's cells. It can happen to anyone. One cigarette company had a very successful commercial in which a rugged, virile cowboy relaxed with a cigarette before riding off into the frontier. Very nostalgic. The actor who portrayed the role died in 1987 from emphysema, often a smoking-related lung disease. Smokers die an average of eight years earlier than nonsmokers.

Smoking decreases stress resistance. Several treatments are available. If you want to manage stress, be nicotine-free.

Moderate or No Drinking (#2). We saw in the last chapter how repeated drinking can lead to alcoholism, and how such alcohol abuse impairs the capacity of the mind and body to function normally. Such disruptions increase life stress, and can lead to the many diseases that we have noted. The increase in stress and the potentially negative consequences occur regardless of the type of alcoholic beverage that you drink. Beer can be just as harmful as hard liquor.

Our society further increases the risks of developing alcoholism. In cultures where alcohol is used at meals or in religious ceremonies, the abuse of alcohol is low. In the United States, however, people tend to drink at the end of the day on an empty stomach, and in settings like cocktail parties where the office pressure is still present. Often people drink by themselves. These drinking patterns have led to high rates of alcohol abuse in our country.

Such abuse is everywhere. At work. At home. At play. A recent study of skiing accidents found that most accidents on the slopes occurred between 2:00 and 3:00 P.M., just after lunch. Forty percent of these accidents were alcohol-related. While some research has demonstrated that moderate drinking may improve health, our societal drinking patterns may lead us to excessive drinking. If, when you drink, you cannot control your drinking, it is better not to use alcohol at all. There are other helpful ways to manage stress and enjoy life.

Sleep (#3). The cultural pressures for us to get ahead in our twenty-four-hour-a-day society tire us out. We need to stop. We need to rest. We need to sleep.

Sleep is important because it heals the minor wear and tear on our bodies each day, and it helps us to consolidate the day's events and preserve them in our memories. Unfortunately, when people are under stress and have too much to do, they often try to get by with less sleep. The restorative and integrating functions of sleep are important tools in managing stress and should not be given up. The average person needs six to eight hours of sleep. Going without sleep does not enhance stress resistance.

Sound Nutrition (#4). What the proper foods are to eat has been a long-standing problem for humans. Quality caloric intake and balance is crucial in keeping the body fine-tuned, so that it is a resource for coping with stress. Obesity is to be avoided if health and well-being are to be attained. There are four known ways to lose weight: diet, exercise, disease, and death. Disease and death are not the answer, so let us turn first to diet, and then to exercise.

One of my students once told me that, if God had wanted us thin, God would have made Sara Lee a carpenter. Notwithstanding the student's wisdom, sensible nutritional habits can enhance our general health and our capacity to cope with life stress.

In general, it is best for us to draw from the four major food groups in developing a balanced diet: dairy products (preferably skimmed); meats, fish, and poultry (preferably lean and skinless); grains, fresh fruits, and vegetables. We want to minimize caffeine, which is a dietary stimulant as we have noted; we want to minimize saturated fats because of the cholesterol problems; and we want to be sure to have enough fiber in our diets. Fiber makes our bowels work properly, appears to minimize contracting colon cancer, and removes wastes from our bodies.

As Lucy in Peanuts would say, "Carrot cake is not a vegetable." Create a balanced diet for yourself, and have everything in moderation.

Breakfast Every Day (#5). Would we expect our cars to work without gasoline? Would we expect our house lights to work without electricity? I suspect we would not, and we should not expect our bodies to work each day without their required energy either.

Research has demonstrated that those men and women who have breakfast each day, who provide their bodies with a source of energy early on have better health and better capacity to cope with life stress. Start your day with the proper nutrients.

Normal Body Weight (#6). Being overweight is often an indicator that the person is consuming more calories than he or she is expending. Many of us are overweight. For both men and women, being very overweight is clearly associated with impaired health. The body is thus not at its best when it is confronted with life

You Are What You Eat.

"No, Gorko, no junk food."

stress. It is important for all of us to work towards maintaining normal body weight or at least not to gain more than we have.

I once treated an elderly woman who was feeling overwhelmed by stress. As part of her treatment, I encouraged her to lose weight by cutting her sweets in half. She assured me that she would do this. The weeks passed with no appreciable weight loss. I inquired again if she was cutting her sweets in half as I had directed. She was, but she was eating both halves. For this person, *desserts* spelled backwards equalled *stressed*.

We attain that normal body weight at age twenty. Here are the formulas for determining normal body weight. For women: height in inches × 3.5 − 108. For men: height in inches × 4 − 128. If, by this formula, you reached your normal body weight by age four, join the rest of the world's dieters.

Regular Exercise (#7). On the phylogenetic scale, we humans are members of the animal kingdom; and, like all animals, we need to exercise. We have shaped our lives, however, into a sedentary state. We drive to work, we sit at a desk, we drive home, we sit in the easy chair, we go to bed. For many of us, our greatest form of exercise is pushing away from the dining room table.

This sedentary life-style is at odds with extensive medical research that finds that persons who exercise regularly have less heart disease, less chance of cancer, and have an increased sense of well-being. Exercise can also improve our endurance and stamina.

Aerobic exercise is exercise for the heart. The heart is a muscle; and, like any muscle, it must be strengthened and kept in good condition. Aerobic exercise (e.g., swimming, jogging) is most helpful if it consists of three twenty-minute periods distributed over seven days. Always warm up and cool down before doing aerobics, and *stop* if you feel pain, faint, or shortness of breath. Some general guidelines for warm-ups and cool-downs may be found in appendix D.

The Institute for Aerobics Research in Dallas, Texas, recently completed a multiyear study of the effects of walking on health. Many of the benefits associated with aerobic exercise can also be obtained by regular walks. If aerobic exercises are not to your liking, you may want to try a walk. Remember to warm-up and cool-down (appendix D). As you begin to feel better, you may even want to try a brisk walk (one mile in fifteen minutes). The more intense the exercise, the greater will be the possible health benefits.

These are seven simple ways to take control of your body to enhance your mastery, and to be better ready to cope with life stress. If you gradually implemented these in your life over a two-year period, you would feel remarkably better. If a male at age forty-five did six or seven of these steps, he would live thirty-three versus twenty-one years longer. That is an *extra decade* of life, and a qualitatively good life at that. If you are female and/or younger, you have even greater possibilities for a longer life. We actually have some control even over how long we might live.

Being alive is very different from being not dead. These seven steps can increase your stress resistance and increase your sense of well-being. You are a good person. Do yourself the favor, and begin to develop these healthy patterns of behavior.

Reasonable Mastery: The Special Problems of Time and Mobility

Time. Fast food, quick sex, instant reservations. The commuter's nanoseconds are never very far away. In our busy lives, time moves quickly. For example, if you drive one hour to work and back each day (two hours round trip), between ages twenty-one and sixty-five, you will spend a full nine years of your life behind the wheel. Almost a decade of your life spent on this one task.

Where does time go? The philosopher, Sebastian de Grazia (1964), has identified five basic types of time. Each of us has essentially one hundred sixty-eight hours of time each week, and we use them in the following five ways. *Work time* is the amount of hours we devote to earning a living through formal paid employment. Forty hours a week is the national standard, although many of us work two jobs for a total greater than forty hours. *Personal time* is the time we spend on the maintenance of our health (sleeping, eating, exercising), the maintenance of the things we own (car repairs, mowing the lawn), and the correcting of other people's mistakes (for example, billing errors on our credit card statement). *Consumption time* is the time we devote to using the goods and services produced by the economy. Time spent watching television, going on vacation, thawing a frozen TV dinner in the microwave. We frequently refer to consumption time as leisure time. As we shall see, it is really misleading to call it such because most people are worn out after their "relaxing" leisure time. *Culture time* is the time any of us devotes to the arts, and *Idleness,* the last form of time, refers to a person who has no work and thus no money for consumption. Unemployed teenagers and some poor elderly can be considered idle people.

As members of a capitalist economic system, we predominantly use work time (to produce goods or services to earn a living) and consumption time (to enjoy the fruits of our labors, and to keep others employed by purchasing what they produce). We also use personal time to maintain ourselves so that we can function in the first two roles. However, there are so many material goods to choose from, and their costs are so expensive that we increase our work time to earn more money. This leaves less time for consumption and personal maintenance time.

How do we cope with this time bind? First of all, we cut back on personal maintenance time. Recall the behavior of our drivers at red lights. Most were engaged in personal maintenance activities: eating, brushing teeth, putting on makeup, and shaving, tasks which there was no time for at home. When most of us are under great stress, we cut back on the very activities that would help us cope more effectively with the stress. We skip meals, sleep less, we don't exercise, and we don't rest. This strategy is akin to taking the engines off the jet aircraft as you taxi down the runway for takeoff.

The second major way we migrants on the road to the good life save time is by consuming several things at once. Instead of doing one activity leisurely during consumption time, we pack in several things at once: watch TV, use the microwave, listen to our latest CD, and read the paper. We work hard at being leisurely (Linder, 1970).

We do this even on vacation. For example, the Edwards family is going on vacation to Cape Cod. They begin their rest by packing every single belonging they have into their minivan: bicycles, beach balls, motor scooters, mopeds, rollerskates, VCR, tape deck, several assorted Walkmans, books, magazines, and last year's *New York Times,* the microwave, the electric can opener, bed linens, dishes, a few assorted kids. To the cottage for a restful week.

They continue their rest by approaching the Cape in a twelve-mile traffic jam at the Sagamore Bridge. When they finally arrive, they clean the cottage, set up house by emptying the car, and begin a piece of madness known only to Americans and completely unintelligible to modern psychology. The rest of the world goes on vacation to rest leisurely, Americans "recharge their batteries." They run.

They run through their "leisure" week. No moment is left unplanned. Several things are done at once. After seeing all the sights on the Cape in one hour and thirty minutes, they eat lunch, swim, play beach ball, catch up on their reading, *and* watch the tide come in. You can hear them: "This is great. This is vacation. We didn't *waste* a minute" (italics mine). Fun!

None of us can have it all. We have seen in chapter 3 that the body does not have the physical energy for such endurance. There are just too many things to do. Now we have seen that there isn't enough time to do it all. The sheer number of decisions to be made in a limited amount of time can lead to irrational behavior, impulse buying, and a general (and correct) feeling of the loss of control of one's life. Set your priorities, limit what you do, keep to your schedule, and leave time for things to go wrong (see Linder, 1970).

Another good way to manage time is to remember that society is a living entity with its own life. Opportunities become available to us if we have reasonable mastery and attachments and are willing to wait. For example, if one seeks to get promoted at work, one would want to stay technically current. However, instead of pushing one's self relentlessly at age twenty-five, it would be helpful to remember that the managers who are now fifty years old will be retiring when this younger employee reaches their current age. Their jobs will then be open. Very often the best way to get ahead is to take your time.

Mobility. While the pursuit of material goods leaves limited time for people, mobility acts directly to disrupt ongoing caring attachments.

As we have seen, the world that you and I take for granted is remarkably different from all that has preceded it in human history in terms of movement. The motor vehicle has freed us. The average person now changes residence eleven times in life. Individuals are uprooted. Families are uprooted. Communities are uprooted. One child goes to college. The second child joins the army. The grandparents go South. The parents hit the road in their Winnebago. A thousand families, a thousand series of uprootings. Only nomads and camel drivers appear to move more than the citizenry of the United States.

The journalist, Vance Packard (1974), has noted that we move to get ahead, to make more money, to claim the prize of a leisurely life, to find new friends and a fresh start. We need to remember, however, that mobility is an isolating act. Like the Farnums in our case example, the individual or the nuclear family moves alone. As such, the movers are cut off from all attachments. Separation and its anxiety must be dealt with. We lose the physiological and psychological benefits from others. Continuous moving, like the Farnums', leads additionally to an abrasiveness toward others, and a general neglect of our homes and communities. Why become involved, if you will only move away? It is too painful to say good-bye again. The social isolation of mobility takes its toll.

In our confusion, we seek attachments where we can. Most people now meet their mates at shopping malls. (Some malls have added nondenominational chapels to expedite things.) Others try single bars or dating services. There are even companies that now rent people just as they rent furniture. Need to make a good impression on your boss? Throw a party, rent your guests.

Clearly, these are not quality caring relationships with the types of helpful exchanges that we noted earlier and that we need for health and well-being. Each of us needs to think through the potential disruptions in attachments that any move we make may entail. In our mobile, fragmented society, it takes a while to find friends and to develop caring attachments. We need to consider the losses as well as the gains. How much? And at what cost?

A Special Word for Those with Burnout

Burnout, as we noted in chapter 1, is that special form of stress that comes from excessive demands by people. In addition to turning on the four components of the stress response, it results further in our psychological withdrawal from these people, and then our denigrating them.

People with burnout need to do some basic things. First, they need to set limits on the amounts of people demands they are confronted with. This can be done by setting limits on the amount of work to be done, by changing the person's job description so that it includes a diversity of tasks, and by going on vacations to be completely free of the people demands for a period of time.

An equally important second antidote to burnout is, paradoxically, people. We have seen in chapter 2 how caring human attachments can improve health and well-being. People with burnout need to avail themselves of this coping resource. Be with people who can be emotionally supportive and provide companionship for you. Not people who will make demands, but people who will provide nurturance. Talk to your colleagues at work about the job's stressors and learn to cope with them, and talk with your friends about life. Do not bring your work problems into your personal, nonwork friendships, and, if you are about to move, consider the move's impact on your caring relationships. Take the time to enjoy with your friends the exciting world about you.

Project SMART: A Place to Begin

Over the years, my patients, my students, and registrants in workshops I have offered for business and professional groups have asked me to find some way for them to get started with all these possible strategies for stress resistance, to help them focus on a manageable place to begin. In response to these requests, I have developed Project SMART.

Project SMART's goals are basic: (1) to reduce life stress by shutting off the stress response; (2) to teach some strategies for reasonable mastery; and (3) if you do this in a group with others, to develop caring attachments. While you could do Project SMART alone, it is more effective and more fun if it is done with others.

Project SMART includes gradual reductions in the dietary stimulants (caffeine, nicotine), relaxation exercises, aerobic exercise, and an approach called stress innoculation in which you can rehearse beforehand better general strategies for solving problems. (Appendix B describes in detail the Project SMART program for health care professionals should they care to offer such a group in their practice.)

To begin this program, gather some of your friends together. Each of you needs to have a physical exam to make sure that your stress symptoms are not some other medical problem, and to be cleared for the aerobic exercise component. Next, all of you will want to read the sections in this book on the stress response and stress-resistant persons. Complete the questionnaires at the back of the book, if you wish, and then you are ready to begin. Group meetings take about one and a half hours each, and you need eight to ten meetings to experience real benefits.

The first meeting is devoted to a general discussion of life stress in our current age. Avoid personal psychological problems; rather, discuss the challenges of daily life facing all of us: incompetent drivers, limited day care, finding a reliable repair person, and the like. The remainder of the first session focuses on the process of how life stress occurs, the four stress-management strategies I have just outlined, and a discussion of the group's general findings on their questionnaires.

The second meeting begins with a general review of managing stress. The group members each choose a dietary stimulant to cut back on; at subsequent meetings they will review their progress in reducing their intake of the stimulant. If one smokes twenty cigarettes a day, he or she should decide to cut back to eighteen. If another member usually has six cups of coffee, he or she should commit to make one of them decaffeinated, and so forth. The changes should be in small, gradual steps to ensure some mastery and to avoid withdrawal symptoms. Caffeine cutbacks should be about twenty-five milligrams of caffeine (generally one cup of coffee or equivalent) each week. The second session closes with the relaxation exercises found in appendix C. You and your friends should sit comfortably in a quiet room where you will be undisturbed for fifteen minutes. In my groups, we measure changes in levels of tension with a very inexpensive biofeedback skin thermometer known as a Biodot. The Biodot changes colors like a mood ring as the person wearing it relaxes. (Biodot International, Inc., PO Box 29099, Indianapolis, IN 46228.) Members should use the relaxation exercises at least once a day. Some members may initially experience temporary light-headedness, tingling, numbness, or warmth in their bodies. These temporary feelings are signs that the body has been very tense, and is beginning to relax. If you feel out of control, or experience intrusive, unpleasant thoughts when you attempt to relax, do not do these exercises. Aerobic exercise, which we shall discuss next, is an equally helpful way to reduce stress, and you will feel more in control.

During the third meeting, members discuss their success in decreasing the intake of whichever dietary stimulant they are focusing on, and they agree to continue. The group then does fifteen minutes of relaxation. The remainder of the time is devoted to selecting some aerobic exercise to be done before the next session. Choose something you would like to do (consistent with any directions from your physician), and begin in small gradual steps. Always do warm-up and cool-down exercises. Appendix D contains instructions for aerobic exercising. Walking is a good form of exercise to start with, if nothing else is appealing. *Stop if you feel faint, are short of breath, or feel pain,* and see your physician if you have any of these problems. The aerobic exercise goal is three twenty-minute sessions over the course of seven days. When each member has made his or her choice for the coming week, the group should warm up, go for a brisk fifteen-minute walk, and then cool down before the session ends. Members do the exercise they have chosen between sessions.

If you are a jogger, it is better to run before 8:00 A.M. or after 6:00 P.M. during the summer to avoid air pollution, especially ozone. If you have panic disorder, do not do aerobic exercises without consulting your physician.

Meetings four through ten follow this basic format: discussion of members' progress in implementing small and increasing reductions of dietary stimulants, relaxation exercises for fifteen minutes, followed by a brisk fifteen-minute walk. (Members are expected to be reducing their intake of dietary stimulants, and performing relaxation and aerobic exercises between sessions.) The remaining time in these sessions is used for stress inoculation.

Stress inoculation is a process that trains individuals in basic strategies for coping with aspects of life stress. Sometimes these strategies include how to be a better listener or how to communicate your affection or concern for another. Often, however, these strategies help us in dealing with noncooperation. Noncooperation is a potentially stressful interaction between two or more people in which at least one person does not care about reaching a reasonable solution to the source of the conflict. It is a normal part of everyday life that we must face and learn to cope with. Practicing how to deal with noncooperation in your Project SMART group can be instructive.

Group members should pick a common stressful problem in living in today's age (again, not highly personal problems). Such problems might include dealing with rush hour traffic, communicating with angry store or bank clerks, or tactfully asserting yourself when individuals cut into a line of people waiting to buy a movie ticket.

The group members then spend time sharing the strategies they would use to solve the problem at hand. Emphasis should be placed on which solution is the best one for the specific person in a specific context. The group needs to pay attention to what verbal messages the person will give, what really needs to be said to get the problem solved, and how this can be communicated tactfully. Members also need to pay attention to the nonverbal communication of the person who is attempting to solve the problem. If you are returning faulty merchandise to a store clerk, in addition to clearly asking for your money back, you need to be able to look the clerk in the eye, stand erect, shoulders back, and speak in a reasonable and audible tone of voice.

Once the verbal communication is clear, and the nonverbal communication is appropriate to the situation, there is one step left. This step is so important that I insist that my group members not practice their answer to the life stress problem on their own until we have completed the last part as a group. In the last part, the members rehearse the problem with all the possible responses the person may encounter when he or she attempts to solve the problem. The possible responses range from cooperation in solving the problem, to cooperation but with anger, to indifference, to hostility, and to complete refusal to cooperate. If the problem is how to deal with the store clerk over faulty goods, some member should role-play the store clerk; another, the customer. They would then practice the varying degrees of cooperation. The remaining group members should offer suggestions for dealing with the various types of noncooperation. Stress inoculation works in a similar manner for situations of expressing caring. (Stress inoculation was developed by a psychologist, Dr. Donald Meichenbaum, 1977, if you wish to read further.)

Project SMART has proven itself helpful in reducing stress overdrive, and in enhancing mastery and attachment (Flannery, 1987). It can be helpful to you also. You can improve your stress resistance by utilizing Project SMART in small gradual steps. If a reasonable trial of Project SMART produces no real beneficial effects, see your physician for further professional help.

7

MASTERY: FINANCIAL DECISIONS

Money isn't the root of all evil. Lack of money is.
—George Bernard Shaw

The mass of men lead lives of quiet desperation.
—Henry David Thoreau

"Don't you *dare* talk to me that way!" she yelled from the other side of the kitchen. "I'll do what I damn well please," he shot back. "Pick, pick, pick, pick. You're as bad as your mother." Fly now, pay later. They had really flown, and now they were paying. They were really paying.

Spring had arrived bright and warm that year. The flowers were especially brilliant in their hues, and formed an unending bouquet for Susan. Everyone had been in agreement that she was an exceptionally elegant bride. Tall, slender, blessed with physical beauty and personal grace, she loved Richard deeply and was freely choosing to spend the rest of her life in his arms. She would do anything for him.

Richard, for his part, was overwhelmed with warmth and gratitude. He had been a gifted athlete and his years in graduate school had prepared him well for his career, and for life. And now he would take a bride. His bride. His Susan. For better or for worse. He too loved her deeply. He too would give her everything he could. Many were the moist eyes in the chapel that day, and envious were some of the hearts.

"Go walk off of a pier." It had come to this. It had taken just five years of married life to exact this bitterness. Credit cards. The plastic was ubiquitous. They had wanted to give each other the best. Gifts were ways of expressing love, were they not? Let every day be Christmas. Charge it.

Somewhere they had lost count, and lost each other. They were several thousands of dollars in debt. "Pick, pick, pick, pick, pick." Richard became depressed. He had never considered Susan and divorce in the same thought until today. In five short years, it had come to this.

How did this happen? How did such a promising beginning go awry? We have noted that lack of money is the most common source of stress in our culture. What happened to Richard and Susan is not uncommon. The present divorce rate in our country is 50 percent, and consumer debt is a leading cause of these break-ups. Why does it happen?

The cause is subtle, but the potential for debt is everywhere so that we gradually accept it as something to be expected. As we have noted earlier, in a market economy personal fulfillment is defined as the amount of material goods a person has. Market economies do not focus on creativity or service to others as primary forms of fulfillment. The emphasis is on material goods. In 1987, the average American spent 97 percent of his or her after-tax income on goods and services. We give gifts to express our love, but we often come to equate the gift or material good with love. We confuse the giver with the gift.

Thoreau wrote that many people lead lives of quiet desperation. In a market economy this desperation can come about because of a lack of money. Without really understanding what they are doing, many people have made major financial decisions before age thirty that have locked them into a lifetime of debt. Steep mortgages, expensive cars, world travel are some common examples. None of us can have it all. As we have seen, we do not have the physical energy for the many choices available to us, and we do not have enough time. We need to add the third factor to that list: most of us do not have enough money to have it all. The result of overspending can be a life of quiet desperation.

The key to financial management is to have a reasonable balance between your income and your level of material expectation. Your income is the amount of cash you earn and take home. Your level of material expectation is how much of the goods and services you want. If your income is higher than your level of material expectations, then you end up saving since you haven't spent all of your income on goods. This is relatively rare in our culture. The opposite situation is more frequent: your level of material expectation exceeds your income. This results in debt. Most Americans compound the problem further by using credit. Instead of lowering our levels of material expectations, we borrow income from others. The debt from our credit and accumulated interest is thus added to the original debt from our income. The stage is set: the lack of money becomes a continuing source of stress.

People initially become agitated and depressed when they owe money. Our market economy being what it is, these same persons consume more to avoid feeling depressed. To do this, however, they have to go further into debt, and the vicious cycle continues. In the course of time, these financial worries can lead to divorce, physical illness, substance abuse, and neglect of loved ones.

I am not advocating that we turn back the clock, and lead lives of deprivation somewhere in the backwoods. The material advances of our age surely can enhance the quality of our lives. We need to find a balance, however, between reasonable mastery and caring attachments, a balance between material goods and time to be with others. This chapter provides an overview of your life's income and the major purchases you may choose to make. It is an attempt to help you find the balance between your income and level of material expectation. Most of the people I have counseled for life stress have no sense of where their money goes. These pages are meant to provide you with a road map before you are halfway along the journey and become lost.

It is a common (and false) assumption in our culture that, if we only make more money, we shall solve the problem. This is not true. As a person's income increases, so does that person's cost of living. As we move higher on the social ladder, our life-style costs more. The amount of illness we have may increase. No matter what our income bracket is, the issue for all of us remains one of finding a balance between income and level of material expectation.

With the exception of excessive debt, there are no right or wrong answers to the basic financial decisions that face all of us. Our goal here is informed choice. We have financial resources to aid us: income, cash, reasonable credit, and equity. We also have nonmonetary resources: time, knowledge, people, and reasonable choice. None of us can have it all, and too much debt is a one-way ticket to the life of quiet desperation. Since debt is the most common source of stress, each of the issues in this chapter can potentially increase or decrease our life stress. We need to think through each one carefully, and make whatever changes seem necessary in small, manageable steps. Caveat emptor. Let us buyers beware.

Making Money

Depending on whose statistics you read, 1 percent of the population owns 34 percent of the wealth, or 6 percent of the population owns 94 percent of the wealth, or 20 percent of the population owns 76 percent of the wealth. Whatever the actual figure, these statistics have two important messages for us: there is a limit to how much money we can make unless we inherit, marry into wealth, or win big in the lottery. Thus, we had better be very good at what we do to earn our living in an increasingly competitive, international marketplace, and equally skilled at saving and making interest.

Organizational stress, or stress at work, is an extensive area of inquiry in its own right, and is beyond the scope of this book with its focus on personal stress-resistance strategies. There are, however, three aspects of our lives in these complex work structures that we can exercise some personal control over to reduce our stress even in the context of a large business. These factors include our competence, our psychological contract, and our monitoring of our job descriptions. We need to find the balance that is best for us in the workplace.

Competence. Employees have one of two strategies to use as members of the work force. One strategy is to rely on competence, the second is to rely on personality. Only the former strategy is usually successful over the longer term (Cherniss, 1980).

Competence very simply is the knowledge and training to do your job to the best of your ability. This means applying yourself to your studies in your formal schooling, and remaining technically competent by upgrading your work skills over the course of your lifetime. Maintaining technical competence will keep you continuously employable, and continually employable in the higher salary ranges.

People who rely on their personality use their youthful energy, charm, charisma, and cheerful presence to curry favor with their colleagues to reduce their work loads, and with their supervisors to enhance their chances for promotion. Since they are often lacking in the technical skills to do their jobs adequately, they become easily bored and begin to focus their energies on their personal life. Today's business world is technically complex and constantly changing, a fact that makes the personality strategy a poor choice for obtaining and maintaining gainful employment. With the possible exception of public relations or retail sales, the personality approach fails because no business can afford an employee who is obsolete.

If you have been using personality as a strategy, move toward competency-based training and obtain supervision as quickly as you can. People who use personality as a work strategy are usually passed over in the labor force by age thirty-five. Excellence becomes its own reward in the marketplace in terms of advancement and earned income.

Your Psychological Contract. You have control of this. Psychologist Harry Levinson (1976) has come up with an interesting idea, the psychological contract. Regardless of your organization's problems and stress, you also have control over your psychological contract. When any of us starts a job, we sign a written contract with our employer to provide a certain type of service each week for a certain salary and benefits. Equally important but unwritten (and often unexpressed) is the individual's psychological expectations about job satisfaction.

Each of us has a vision about how we would function best in our profession or trade. It includes our vision of how we can be at our best in the workplace: the skills in ourselves we value most (such as research, teaching, service delivery, marketing); the setting we would like (small company, Fortune 500 corporation, self-employment); the income level we hope to attain, and the working conditions we view as acceptable (plush office suite, working among the poor).

This vision also includes the primary reasons we are motivated to work hard and remain productive. The reasons vary for each of us. Some common ones include caring for others, making friends, financial security, flexible working hours, benefits, being at the cutting edge of the advances in one's career area, prestige, and so forth.

When you and I go to work, in addition to our written contract with our employer, we have an unwritten psychological contract with the company to provide us the environment and opportunities to develop our vision of our work selves. As long as the company is providing the opportunities to grow at work as we wish, there is minimal stress, and we remain motivated, productive, and generally content. When our jobs are at great variance with our vision, life stress follows. For example, if you really enjoy sales and marketing, but your company put you in charge of production, your psychological contract would probably be broken. If your reason for working is to be at the cutting edge of advances in your field, and your company drops its research and development division and falls behind in the field, your psychological contract would again be broken.

You have some control over the kind of stress at work if you know clearly what your psychological work needs are. Sometimes a change in job description or transfer to a different part of the company can resolve the problem. Sometimes a new and different job is the best answer. You will remain unmotivated to do your best, regardless of how much you are paid, until the needs of your psychological contract are met. (See Levinson, 1976, if you wish to read further.)

Your Job Description. Cherniss (1980) has written one of the better books on stress in the workplace. He found that one of the most common sources of stress at work is unclear job descriptions. Rarely are job descriptions written in enough detail to prevent problems for the company. Such descriptions are usually brief, listing the tasks to be done, but offering no help in how to get these tasks done in the organization setting. You have some control over this source of stress if you understand where you are encountering system conflicts.

Some conflicts arise from overload, having too much to do. This can happen if a company grows very quickly or, conversely, if mergers and layoffs occur. Conflicts can also arise from mixed messages from two or more supervisors. One supervisor says to have your reports done; another supervisor says to concentrate on sales first. Conflicts can also arise when there is a difference between your basic values and company policy. This is particularly true if you feel the company is not being honest with its customers, or is placing them at risk for harm. Conflicts may arise if you have no sense of how your job contributes to the overall mission of the organization, and/or if you have no sense of the mission or purpose of the company. In situations like these, employees operate in a state of confusion. Finally, conflicts can arise if you are working well below your capabilities and are bored by repetitive tasks.

If you are feeling stress at work, but you know that you are competent, and that your basic psychological contract is valid, then it is usually helpful to assess where things may be at odds in your job description. Think out clearly what you are supposed to be doing. Start with the first step of your task, and closely evaluate each step in the process until it is blocked from successful completion. From the listing above, come to some understanding of why it is blocked and what you might need for assistance to resolve the conflict. Then go to your supervisor.

Do not assume that your employer knows the details of your work responsibilities. He or she is dealing with production schedules, budget processes, and staffing issues among other things. If your supervisor is not approachable, you may choose to live with the problem. If your supervisor is approachable, however, tactfully alert him or her to the problem and share your suggestions for a possible solution. A successful resolution to the conflict is good for the company because you remain highly productive. It is good for you because it reduces your work stress. It is good for your boss because there is one less problem for him or her to have to deal with.

Some problems at work are beyond your control and that of your supervisor. The national debt, certain advances in technology, state and local taxes are examples of issues usually beyond immediate control. Exercise careful judgment in determining whether the conflict can be solved at the employee level.

A special word for women who are reading this book. If you have never participated in competitive athletics or been in formal military service, you may be at a distinct disadvantage in the workplace. Conflicts may arise for women because business runs on the rules of athletic competition and the army, and women may not understand the unwritten rules. For example, do you understand the expressions: "We'll go up the middle," or "Let's go off tackle?" If not, it may be helpful to you to read *Games Your*

Mother Never Taught You (Harragan, 1977) or to play tag football with the kids in the neighborhood. These are good ways to learn the unwritten rules quickly.

Money Matters Needn't Be Distasteful.

Spending Money

Now that you have an income, you need to think about how to utilize those earnings with a reasonable level of material expectation to avoid excessive debt and a life of quiet desperation. This is especially true in marriage. Marriage has great potential for reducing life stress, but we also know that consumer debt is a leading source of divorce.

Let us begin with some general guidelines:

Be Informed. In twenty years of counseling, I have encountered many persons who were stressed because they had no understanding of general finances, the tax code, the legal and judicial systems, the stock market, and even how their own government works at the local and national levels. These individuals have gone into debt when they did not have to, they have spent money they could have easily saved, and they had no sense of how to seek recourse in the legal and governmental institutions made available by their tax dollars.

Thus, the first rule of money management is to be informed.

There are several excellent books on the topics I have listed above. Read. Become informed. It will cost you a lot of money in your lifetime if you do not understand how our country's economy works. If you do not understand the tax laws in a general way, for example, you will never be able to make fully informed financial choices.

Students often ask me why I insist on reading in a video age. Such a view has greatly underestimated the power of the computer. In our day and age, information is the base of knowledge, and information with informed judgment is power. Computers are the major source of information in our society, and a computer printout is a printed page, not a video picture. Those in the "know" have the power to shape events for their own well-being, and those in the know realize the importance of reading. To reduce life stress, gather information and remain informed.

Money Management: Five Basic Steps. There are some basic steps that can be helpful to each of us over the course of our lives as we attempt to make general sense out of the chaos in the marketplace. Since most of us will not win the lottery, we need to think about getting rich *slowly*. Following these five basic steps and having a reasonable level of material expectation will greatly enhance the quality of your life by reducing financial stress. Here is the strategy:

(1) *Save*. To be financially successful all of us need to save some of our income. Consistent saving puts you ahead in financial matters because most Americans save only 3 to 4 percent of their after-tax income. As your savings accumulate, people will pay you money to borrow your savings for their excessive consumption.

Most Americans not only do not save but consume even more by borrowing. If you are wise, you will quickly learn that by not using credit cards excessively and by paying the bill in full at the end of the billing period, you will have avoided an 18 percent cost on your investment. By having savings, you can afford to pay the principle at the end of the month and avoid the credit charges. Why give your money to someone else when you don't have to?

(2) *Invest*. Gain even further monies by investing your savings in some financial strategy that will yield the highest return for you. Depending on income and tax bracket, there are opportunities like Treasury bills, state and municipal bonds, certificates of deposit, money-market funds, and the stock market. The more informed

you are, the greater will be your opportunities for choice. Aside from some monies you have immediately available for rainy days, you are generally not maximizing your return in a regular bank passbook account. Find better returns for your investment, but never invest in a financial arrangement that keeps you up at night worrying. It is not worth the toll on your health.

(3) *Spend Wisely.* Having saved and invested your money at good interest rates, you are now ready to purchase what you want. Review your income level, make sure that your level of material expectation is reasonable, and then purchase what you need and want. A helpful general spending strategy is to make your purchases by using only your wages and the interest monies that you have accrued. Try to leave your principal intact as much as possible.

(4) *Purchase Sensibly.* There is a man in our neighborhood who spent close to three hundred dollars on a deluxe charcoal-burning, self-starting, self-cleaning, chrome-finished outdoor grill. Three times each year, he cooks six patties of ninety-nine-cent hamburger. Are the flames brighter? Is the meat more tasty? This thinking is typical of many of us. We become mesmerized by the advertising, and we buy "deluxe" for the sake of buying "deluxe." A better rule of thumb is to purchase those things that will make you happy, but leave time for comparison shopping so that you can purchase the most durable product at the lowest price.

(5) *Limit Credit Card Use.* Excess credit card debt is a major source of life stress in our country. In truth, you only need one major bank credit card (e.g., Visa, Mastercard) to establish a credit rating. One card can also serve as a self-policing mechanism as it can help to keep you from charging everything in sight. People who charge many things each day lose track of how much they have gone into debt by the end of the month. This is how the credit card debt problem begins. It is not usually the major purchase that you have thought through; it is the small purchases that you don't keep track of. Some stores, such as major department stores, are not even really interested in what you purchase. They earn more money from your cedit card interest payments. (One large department store even has credit cards for children as young as two years of age.)

As a general rule of thumb, no more than 20 percent of your monthly take-home pay should be spent on charges. If you are stalling one creditor to pay another, or have a lot of past-due bills, you are in trouble. Recognize these signs for what they are. Limit your charges, pay for some purchases in cash, and plan ahead. If you are in severe debt, avoid consolidation loans. Go to your local Better Business Bureau for credit card counseling. They will work out a plan with your creditors to help solve your financial life stress.

In all of this, we need to remember that material goods will not replace caring attachments as resources for health and well-being.

Major Financial Decisions

Now that we have reviewed the basics of money management, we need to turn our attention to the major financial decisions that most of us will make in our lifetimes. In my years of practice, I have seen men and women of all ages under severe financial stress because they never had an overview of their finances. In particular, they have little awareness of how each major financial decision affected their lives in the long term. The goal here is for all of us to have such a general overview of our financial position for a lifetime. We shall look at both income and expenditures involving the major financial decisions for most people: shelter, children, education, transportation. These decisions are not solely financial, but money is a central part of each of them. Poor decisions lead to frustration, and there are many examples of financially strapped parents abusing their children or abusing themselves with alcohol or drugs.

In the example to follow, I have chosen a middle-class or upper middle-class couple with two children. They live in an urban environment on the East Coast. Since salaries and expenses differ by regions and states, you will need to develop your own figures based on your own local conditions. My primary goal is to help you focus your understanding on your lifetime so that, whatever decisions you make, those decisions will be carefully considered and result in decreased life stress.

Salaried Income. How much can one expect to earn in a lifetime working career of forty years? In the early years, your salary will be lower, and later it will be higher (but so will the cost of living). In 1989 dollars, an average salary was $36,000 per year. As you can see in table 1, over forty years this comes to $1,440,000. If you are married, and your spouse is in the paid labor force for some of

Table 1

Average Lifetime Finances:

Salaried Incomes:		Costs:	
First Spouse —	$1,440,000	Home	$504,000
Second Spouse —	540,000	Raising Two Children	240,000
	$1,980,000	College	192,000
		Motor Vehicles	168,000
		Operating Costs	168,000
		Miscellaneous	
		Income Taxes	540,000
		Heating	69,600
		Electricity	20,160
		Telephone	11,520
		Food	312,000
			$2,245,280
		Debit:	$265,280

these years, family income will be greater. I have assumed the spouse (male or female) to be in the paid labor force for thirty years at a salary of $18,000 per year.

The spouse's salary in those thirty years would equal $540,000 for a total family income of $1,980,000. With reasonable financial planning, this would seem to be enough income for a comfortable life. If your salaried income is higher, remember that your costs are commensurately greater because society has higher expectations of you. If your spouse returns to the labor force during the preschool years of any children you may have, salary income will increase but day-care costs will need to be subtracted from income ($3,120 yearly).

Shelter. To rent or buy is the basic question each of us must face. The psychological reasons that inform this financial decision vary greatly. People buy houses for psychological stability, for a yard for the children, as a symbol of family life, as an investment, as a forced savings account through mortgage payments, and so forth. Others rent because they want the freedom to come and go as they wish, because they do not want their time or money tied up in the care and upkeep of a house. In fact, some individuals whose own childhood family homes were unhappy often avoid buying a home because it reminds them of past unpleasantness.

Table 2 presents the financial considerations in renting versus buying. People who choose to rent must also have a savings plan if they are to avoid financial stress later on. The home owner has an investment that frequently (but not always) appreciates in value, and the home owner usually has tax benefits. However, in addition to principal/interest/taxes (three times the original purchase price of the house over the thirty years of the mortgage), the home owner must add house insurance costs, maintenance costs (e.g., painting the house every five years), replacement costs (e.g., a new roof every twenty years), the amount of personal time involved in the house's upkeep (mowing lawn, fixing faucets, interior cleaning) unless you enjoy such things, increased medical bills from carrying a mortgage, and less time and freedom. For most home owners this is a major financial and time commitment for over twenty-five to thirty years. Persons who purchase condo units need to remember that in addition to buying housing, there is a rental fee (condo fee) plus limited freedom to do as you wish with the unit you own. Decisions about shelter should not be made lightly in today's housing market.

Our couple decided to buy the 1989 average priced house at $168,000, which means the house will cost $504,000 for principal, interest, and taxes for thirty years. This means that they will pay $336,000 of their income for the mortgage and municipal taxes. This money will not be available for other purchases unless they take out a second mortgage at additional cost. The cost of the house is noted in table 1.

Children. This couple, like most average couples, will have two, possibly three children. Although children give expression to our love, and continue the human family, having children is also in part a twenty-year financial decision. It costs about $120,000 per child for the first eighteen years of their lives (somewhat more for female than male offspring). Since most families are upwardly mobile, they want their children to have a college education. Collegiate expenses include tuition, room and board, books, haircuts, clothes, spending money, and air fare home during school breaks. This comes to about $24,000 per year per child for private schooling. Our couple

Table 2

Shelter: To Rent or To Buy?

		Home
Renting		Principal/Interest/Taxes, House Insurance,
+	versus	Maintenance Costs, Replacement Costs, Possible Home Owner's Time, Increased
Savings		Medical Bills, Less Freedom, but Tax Benefits

chose to send their two children to college for a total child rearing cost of $192,000. These costs are noted in table 1.

Several issues about children recur in our culture, and I have seen them often in my years of counseling. Since children are a major financial undertaking, it is worth thinking about them for a moment. Is it unnatural for adults not to want children? No. Some people's own childhoods were unhappy, and they may not want children themselves. Others as teenagers may have been responsible for siblings because of parental illness, and they may want to do something different with their adult years. Others appear to be born with different interests, and have no interest in children in much the same way you and I may not have an interest in music or French.

Should you have a child to save a marriage? No. There are many good reasons to have children, but to save a troubled marriage is usually not one of them. If the adult relationship is already weakened, the stress of a child will tear it apart. Should you have a child for companionship in your old age? Again, probably not. Our society is too mobile for you to assume that your children will be nearby in your later years. Should you have a child to keep you from being lonely? No. Loneliness is usually a problem inside the person, and adding another person will not necessarily solve the problem (see chapter 10). Should you have a child to prove that you can do it? No. You may like eggs for breakfast, but I'll bet you never wanted to be a hen. None of us can have it all.

Motor Vehicles. Our average couple will buy about one car at $12,000 every five years for forty years. If the spouse enters the labor force, the spouse will also probably purchase a new car every five years. The cost for these cars will be $168,000. In addition, fuel, insurance, taxes, and maintenance of these vehicles will be about $2,400 per car per year. For seventy years of driving these costs come to an additional $168,000, and these figures have been added to table 1.

Two things to bear in mind. First, if you drive a subcompact car, your chances of being killed in a car accident are seven times higher than in a compact or larger size car. Is it worth the initial savings? Second, the Hertz Corporation estimates that if you traded in your car every ten years rather than the five year average, you would realize a savings of $20,400, money that you could spend on other things.

Miscellaneous. There are other basic costs our salaried couple can expect to incur. This couple in their tax bracket will pay about $540,000 in personal income taxes. (The mortgage tax deduction reduces their taxes from the 28 percent bracket to the 25 percent bracket.) Heating and air conditioning costs for forty years would be about $69,000; electricity, about $20,160; telephone, about $11,520; health insurance for the family would be about $20,000 over these same years, and food at $180 per week would be $312,000 over the same time span.

If we turn now to table 1 and compare costs with salaried income, we can see that this couple will be in debt for much of their married life. We have not included the costs of clothing, recreation, vacations, emergency reserves, nor any credit card interest for purchases not made outright. (Nor have we included the $4,000 cost for burial from worrying about all these expenses.) There is not enough money for all of us to have it all. The sad truth is that many couples today must choose between children and home ownership.

This debt outcome could be altered by inheritance monies or some form of savings, and the monies for college would be more available if the couple put money aside for this right after their marriage.

Some of this couple's commitments need not have been undertaken, others could be modified. The purpose of this exercise has been to demonstrate the impact of finances over a lifetime. We have choices, and, if we understand the larger impact of our decisions, a life of desperation need not be our lot.

Keeping Money

Finally, we need to turn our attention to life's inevitable rainy days and to our retirement. All of us need to plan for these events as we go along in life.

The considered wisdom is that we need to set aside $5,000 in immediately available cash reserves for day-to-day crises. We need money to fix the furnace, money for sudden illness, money for car repairs. In addition, in planning for rainy days, we should set aside the equivalent of six months of our income in relatively liquid assets (bonds, certificates of deposit) for sudden illness or unemployment.

The second major reason for saving money is for retirement. Since it is possible that the Social Security system may not be able to fully support all of the nation's retirees by the year AD 2000, we need to have additional retirement strategies. Pensions, IRAs, Keogh Plans, equity in property, stocks, and bonds are all possible avenues to explore.

With reasonable financial forethought, each of us can exercise some reasonable mastery over the financial life stress that we can expect to encounter in our lives.

8

ATTACHMENTS: MAKING RELATIONSHIPS WORK

There must be more to life than having everything.
—Stendhal

There is this whole—you and I.
—Dr. Tom Dooley

Stale smoke filled the empty silence of the night. He pulled up his pants, mumbled good night to Kate, and headed aimlessly towards his car. Disgust and self-rebuke had become his bodyguards.

At forty-three, James was restless, agitated—angry really. He also had this continuous desire to make love. At times he could taste it, yet sex itself brought no relief for his desire. He could make no sense of it. He was bored, he felt taken for granted, and his twenty years of work seemed irrelevant and devoid of meaning. Wasted time. Surely, life must offer something more than monotony.

At first, it seemed plausible enough. He certainly wouldn't be the first person to have an affair. He felt entitled to some sort of reward. Sex and the excitement of an illicit rendezvous seemed like it might be just what the doctor ordered. But that was then, and now was now. Two-and-a-half years later, with twenty-five-year-old Kate as his third partner, he was still angry, still tumescent, still confused. Something was missing.

Paula was no ordinary woman, he thought, as he drove home. They had had a reasonable life together. It had had its ups and downs, but so did any marriage. She was a good woman, a loyal wife, hardworking. Why did he cheat on her? He certainly didn't feel any better for having done so. His kids were basically good kids, although he was tired from all his overtime at work to come up with forty thousand dollars every year for two college tuitions. He'd be glad to have that monkey off his back.

He lit a cigarette, spent some time thinking up what his excuse would be this night. (Did Paula know or at least suspect?) How could he explain this to her? He didn't understand it himself. He knew the anger had started three years before when his father died. That anger was more his mistress than Kate would ever be. But why did people have affairs? He took another drag on his cigarette, and drove on into the darkness, his darkness.

We have seen in chapter 4 how caring relationships with others help to reduce life stress, and increase our sense of health and well-being. The benefits from caring relationships such as improved cardiac and immune system functioning are not insignificant. Such benefits are especially possible in a good marriage. This chapter focuses on what makes adult relationships, including marriage, workable and pleasant. Since there are several people like James and Paula who are having affairs that do not make them happy, this chapter will also focus on where human relationships may go awry so that we can learn how to develop the best of caring attachments to others.

Depending on which set of statistics we wish to accept as accurate, somewhere between 28 to 70 percent of all married men and women have had affairs. As we have noted, affairs are a leading cause of divorce along with consumer debt and alcohol abuse. Many of those who divorce remarry only to divorce again.

Interest in affairs, sex, and things sexual saturates our daily lives. Television and radio stations broadcast problems having to do with some aspect of sex to ensure high ratings. Our national advertising abounds with sexual innuendo. Bumper stickers on half of the cars in the United States proclaim how one group does it better than another.

Many could be and are like James, unfaithful and confused. He asks an important question for all of us: Why do people have affairs? Has married life as an institution failed? Is the need for sex so great? Is this the New Revolution? It is my belief that affairs represent an attempt to form attachments in an age that has over-emphasized mastery. I also believe that such affairs are failed attempts for reasons that are important for us to understand. Our sense of health and well-being depend on it.

The General Nature of Adult Relationships

What Relationships Are Not

Let us begin by briefly noting two common, but equally inaccurate views of relationships:

Relationships are not primarily sexual. Sex, sex, some nudity, total nudity. I suspect now that I have your undivided attention. The reason most of us pay attention to things sexual is that sexual activity and orgasms are the highest form of intense biological pleasure for most humans. Having stated this, if I were then to say to you that sex does not make a whole human relationship, most of you would agree. You might add additional relationship factors like mutual respect, caring, help in times of crisis. Even though we know in our minds that human relationships are not primarily sexual, in our culture we sometimes act as if they were. This overemphasis on sexuality is in part created by our national advertising. Material goods in our society are often sold by means of a sexual theme, and such advertisements are found in the pages of our most reputable magazines and newspapers.

The product to be sold is paired with sexual symbols, the symbols of intense biological pleasure. Then the product becomes pleasurable in its own right because of such an association. This type of advertising appears to work very well. Reflect on how we pursue material goods with such a national tenacity. Sex in advertising is a part of why we may buy more than we need.

Such an approach has its downside, however. First, it colors our expectations about material goods; we expect them to provide the same pleasure as sex. Use toothpaste X, and the world's greatest lover will ring your doorbell. Second, even though we know that human relationships involve more than sex, the effect of the continuing sexual messages in our advertising tends to reduce our view of human encounters to a basic sexual goal. In the ads, love equals sex. It dehumanizes our encounters with others. Even though we know sex by itself cannot sustain a relationship, we may begin to act as if it can. We behave as if sex equals love. Such an attitude is part of the reason for so many divorces and so many affairs. Relationships are not primarily sexual.

Relationships are not material goods. This is the second inaccurate view of relationships, and again, most of us would find this statement to be patently obvious. There are, however, also powerful attitudes in our culture about material goods that influence our perception of human relationships.

With continuous change as a given in our technological society, many manufacturers are attempting to keep pace by creating modular components. Modular design creates a product with a series of interchangeable parts so that, if there are engineering advances, only one piece or module needs to be replaced instead of the whole unit. Desktop computers and home sound systems are examples of modular products.

A second important aspect of material goods is planned obsolescence. Since manufacturers need people to buy their products, they build them to break down after a certain period of time. They plan and build the product to fail and become obsolete in the hope that you and I will replace it. For example, you buy a moderately priced watch that is guaranteed for twelve months, but may be built to fail in eighteen months. When it fails, the expectation is that you will throw it away rather than repair it, and buy another watch made by the same company.

While modular components and planned obsolescence may sell material goods, like the sexuality in advertising, these concepts may begin to affect our view of human relationships.

Some of us refrain from forming close relationships in part because we see people as being replaceable as if they were modular units. If we then add in the variant of planned obsolescence, when a relationship is in difficulty, we don't repair it. We throw it away. We divorce. We have affairs. We pack up and leave. To be sure, the reasons for these decisions are much more complex, but in part our attitudes toward material goods generalize to our view of people. Human relationships are not the same as material goods.

What Relationships Can Be

What then are the true signs of healthy relationships?

Caring human relationships can greatly aid in our health and well-being, and, in spite of the rate of change in our industrial/ corporate world, there are some basic characteristics that can facilitate the development and sustaining of caring attachments even in this day and age of seeming impermanence. These are the characteristics often utilized by stress-resistant persons in their efforts to care for others.

Trust. We have already discussed this sine qua non of human encounters. For a relationship to endure, there must be predictable behavior and similar values in both parties. To this, we now need to add one additional aspect. The similar values that the parties espouse must leave time for caring attachments. If the values held jointly overemphasize the pursuit of material goods and excessive mastery, the relationship is at higher risk of failing because the parties have left no time for each other nor the time needed for the development of trust.

Mutual Respect. For a caring relationship to work, each party needs a basic respect for the welfare of the other, a desire not to intentionally harm the other either physically or psychologically, and a wish to see the other grow fully according to the other's gifts and talents. The Golden Rule of treating others the way you would wish to be treated is a concise way to remember this. A person in such a relationship needs to respect the other's competence, to share resources for problem solving, and to be willing to compromise.

Relationships that feature arrangements like prenuptial agreements, two separate bank accounts, specifically stated nights out alone, and a legal division of household tasks, including who is to do the dishes on what night, may sometimes be devoid of the mutual respect and compromise that are essential to the growth of attachments. Each dyad must consider such decisions carefully. For relationships to work, mutual respect must be part of the process.

Communication. We live in a fast-paced world. Both the world and those of us in it are constantly changing, so it should not surprise us that we could easily lose track of each other. This losing track occurs often with people we see infrequently, but it sometimes happens even with those we live with daily.

When I do couples counseling or family work, I often ask one party involved to state two sentences, and then I have the others repeat the sentences back verbatim, and tell the speaker what he or she meant. This is a simple way to demonstrate how difficult it is to communicate clearly in our industrial age. With some practice communication skills can improve.

We should expect change, and we should expect misunderstandings in such a complex world as ours. Communication is so important that I often assign as homework an exercise in which the couple or family set aside one-half hour each day to communicate what is happening in their lives. It greatly reduces misunderstandings and hurt feelings. It also reduces life stress because it allows for planning in advance, and resolving disagreements early on.

A second common homework assignment I give for enhancing communication is to encourage the couple or family to set aside time each evening to thank each other for the helpful things they have done that day. Thank you for making breakfast. Thank you for working at the job that is so burdensome. Thank you for taking us for ice cream. Some people feel awkward at first in saying thank you, but it quickly becomes more tolerable. These thank you's enhance communication about how helpful we are to each other. They keep us from taking each other for granted, and they increase our mutual respect.

Shared Economic Responsibility. In any relationship there is some need for monies—whether it's taking your best friend for coffee, raising children, buying a home, or career development with one's spouse or significant other. Each of these activities necessitates some sharing of economic resources. Since lack of money is the most common source of life stress, and since consumer debt is one leading cause of divorce, in any relationship the amount of income and the parties' levels of material expectation need to be thought out. Debt should be kept to a minimum.

Economic resources may include other factors besides income. One spouse remaining at home to raise children provides important labor and financial savings in the unpaid labor force (no day care costs, houses cleaned, meals prepared, etc.). Similarly, the do-it-yourself home repair project, business entertainment at home rather than in restaurants, baby-sitting the neighbor's child are all examples of similar economic resources.

Relationships that ignore sharing economic resources and responsibilities do so at peril. Individuals may give more or less at different points in the relationship, but there should be some sense of balance and reciprocity. One should not be afraid to raise the issue of distribution of responsibilities tactfully if one party does not feel the sharing is equal.

Time. If you have read these previous four items and wondered who has time for such things, your relationships may be at risk. There is neither physical energy, money, nor time to have all of our potential material goods as we have seen in earlier chapters. We need to make time for caring relationships. We must all find some balance between mastery in the pursuit of material goods and the development of caring attachments.

To maintain a good relationship, elements like trust, mutual respect, and communication take time to develop. In addition, we need continuing time to keep abreast of the changes occurring in those relationships. Working sixteen hour days and seven day weeks, having commuter marriages where the spouses travel six or seven hundred miles one weekend a month to be together, developing your professional career by attending the nightly cocktail circuit, being leaders in volunteer community activities—all are examples of how we may place our relationships at risk because we have not allotted time for the task of developing caring attachments. With the divorce rate in our country at 50 percent, we cannot afford not to find the time.

Any relationship will be strained by the allocation of too little time. We need to remind ourselves that caring attachments are necessary for reducing life stress, and for maintaining well-being. We need to plan our time accordingly.

Marriage: The Special Adult Relationship

Coupling seems to be a naturally occurring phenomenon, and a stable marriage contributes markedly to decreased stress and improved health, well-being, and longevity. It is important then for us to understand what makes a marriage work. What is the psychology of marriage? How are people drawn together? What do men and women look for in each other? Why are there so many affairs? We need to understand more fully the power for good of marriage.

Why People Marry. In the early days of human history before AD 1900, people married to ensure physical survival in the face of the daily enemy, death. In recent history, however, other reasons for marriage, including emotional support, intimacy, friendship, and self-esteem, have been added to the list.

Lederer and Jackson (1968) have compiled a fairly representative list of the reasons people marry. Some of the more common ones include: to love another, to improve one's self, to provide for a secure economic future, to increase self-esteem, to meet parental or societal expectations, to avoid the fear of being abandoned, to reduce loneliness, and to get out of the house. I have listed the reasons in descending order from the better reasons to the less helpful ones. Many of us marry for several reasons, and no specific one ensures the marriage will last. As a general rule of thumb, however, if we marry for the less-helpful reasons, it will require greater effort to ensure the viability and success of the marriage because the parties usually have less skills for mastery and for forming caring attachments.

What Men and Women Look for in a Partner. The attributes that men and women seek in each other are as varied as there are individuals seeking them. What we look for seems to change over the course of our lifespan. At twenty, we may seek a partner who is sexually exciting and also a good listener. At fifty, we may seek a partner who is warm, supportive, and compassionate. Even though our needs change with time, there appear to be some common enduring factors.

Men often look for partners who are intelligent and self-reliant, and who have physical beauty and are sexually exciting. (For men, sex is not only physically pleasurable, but also one of the few culturally permissible ways for men to be physically touched.) Because of the economic changes in our society, more and more men are looking for a woman who has good employment skills and who can help out financially. Men also look for partners who can provide companionship and emotional support, and for a person who will appreciate them. Giving a male milk and cookies and listening to him is a sure way to win a friend.

For their part, women may look for men who are intellectually bright, good looking, educated, and have a good income so that they can be assured of protection and reasonable access to material goods and social resources in the culture. For women who work, this second income may further enhance their own quality of life and independence. Generosity seems especially prized by women who wish to have children.

None of us has all of these attributes in their highest form. We also need to understand that several of these factors, not just one, usually determines the marriage choice. Each of us has different strengths to offer in our search for a mate.

The Marriage Itself. Having some sense of why we want to

marry, and having found a partner with the characteristics we value, we are ready for marriage itself. When we exchange vows, we begin a bonding process that can potentially provide the marriage with lifelong stability and strength.

Short-Term/Long-Term Bonding. Sager (1979) has pointed out that, as we grow up, we develop in our minds the concept of the person we would like to marry. This perception is our marriage ego ideal: our vision of the perfect spouse. It is drawn from our experiences with members of the opposite sex. It can include teachers, parents, neighbors, national figures, and so forth. We put together the best of all of these attributes, and the result is our marriage ego ideal. It is largely an unconscious experience, but it does influence which characteristics we seek in our partners. When we marry, we in large part marry our ego ideal. We imagine our partner to have those characteristics we most prize.

Short-term bonding refers to the early period of intense sexual excitement and joy. Many couples describe this as a period of ecstasy. Reason gives way to instinct. The world appears brighter and more exciting. Life is buoyant and fun; the travails of life seem suspended in time. This period can last anywhere from six months to as long as three years. One's marriage ego ideal and the state of ecstasy color our perceptions of everything, including our partner.

Then the shell begins to crack in little ways. Things don't run quite as smoothly as they did. She doesn't seem so beautiful in curlers, he doesn't pick up his socks. The honeymoon is coming to a close, and the couple shifts to long-term bonding. During this process we learn repeatedly that one's spouse does not fit one's ego ideal perfectly. We differentiate our marriage ego ideal from the real person that we married. We learn to assess accurately each other's strengths and weaknesses as a couple. The major task in long-term bonding is to accept the limitations, the strengths, and get on with life. It is during this period that the couple needs to concentrate fully on the characteristics we have noted for stable adult relationships: trust, mutual respect, communication, shared economic responsibilities, and the allotment of time for these things to occur. Successful completion of these tasks can lead to a stable and happy married life.

Marriage Styles. Sager (1979) has also spent many years studying couples. He has noticed that couples develop certain styles of

A Stable Marriage Is A Source of Health.

DRAWN BY HOFF   THE SATURDAY EVENING POST

"Will you stop referring to our anniversaries as 'rounds'?"

interacting in their married years. Most styles are self-explanatory. When both partners agree and then behave as equals, there is equal division of money, chores, and responsibilities. Attempts are made to keep everything evenly divided. Romantic couples have their heads in the clouds. He brings flowers, she makes his special dessert. Life is perpetually rosy and semimystical. Parent couples, as you would guess, are authoritarian, and order each other to do what they feel is best. Children couples, on the other hand, shrink from giving direct orders, and wait quietly and deferentially to see what will happen. Companionates are usually older people whose marriages are contracted primarily for companionship in one's later years. Rationals form a couple where expressing feelings of affection or anger, etc., is very low; the emphasis is on rational thought. These couples are loyal and loving, but they prize reason as a way of resolving marriage issues. Parallels are couples that interact in very limited ways. They do love each other, but they work in tandem and keep their distance from each other.

None of these marriage styles is any better or worse than any other. It is what kind of style works for each couple that is important. We need to remember, however, that since marriage is a changing entity, sometimes individual spouses in a marriage change or outgrow their initial chosen style. If a male child wanted to become a male parent, and the female was content to remain a child, little life stress would follow. However, you can begin to imagine what would happen if a parallel decided to become a romantic while the other partner stayed parallel, or if one romantic adopted a rational style while the other remained a romantic. Life stress would increase. As with other aspects of life we should not be startled by change. If the couple is following the basic five steps for making an adult relationship work, they will find ways to adjust to the change, and to reduce life stress.

Marriage Myths

There are some myths in our culture about successful marriage that are commonly seen by those of us in clinical practice. The myths are false. Since they arise often, it is important to understand that the suggested cultural solutions only increase life stress.

The first myth is that having a child will save a marriage. We have spoken of this earlier. The extra life stress of a child will swamp an already weakened relationship. A second false assumption is that hard times always bring the spouses closer together. This is not necessarily true either. If life events have taxed the couple's resources for coping adequately, the wear and tear may drive them apart. Having friends and neighbors with additional resources can sometimes soften the impact of such painful events, but not always. A third and usually false cultural assumption is that marriage will curtail the drug or alcohol abuse of the partner. Substance abuse is a medical disease, and is no more cured by marriage than is arthritis or diabetes. Have your potential partner find treatment first. It is wiser not to marry until the treated partner has two full years of sobriety, since it can take as long as eighteen months for body chemistry to return to full normality in some substance abusers. A fourth myth is that divorce is a new beginning. This is not necessarily so. The first marriage probably failed because of some fundamental and ineffective way of coping with marital life stress. If a better strategy is not learned, the poor coping style will again disrupt the second marriage. Better to find the ineffective coping strategy and solve that problem first, and then to remarry.

The Nature of Affairs

What is an affair? Based on my twenty years of counseling individuals with this problem, an affair is probably best described as sex outside of the marriage relationship by one or both spouses to meet emotional needs that are usually *not sexual*. While biological appetite may lead to some brief encounters, affairs usually are of longer duration and occur for a variety of differing psychological needs. Over the years I have found the reasons for such affairs to vary greatly. Sometimes it is for excitement to relieve the boredom of daily routines. Sometimes it is to increase self-esteem or to communicate anger to the spouse over some other unresolved issue in the marriage. Sometimes it is for solace and self-soothing in the face of pain or sadness. At times, it is a way of avoiding true caring attachments to others. The reasons vary, but sex per se is often not the main consideration. In fact, in most affairs, the sexual activity itself occupies only a small percentage of the time the couple spends together.

A common example of an affair motivated by the presence of unmet emotional needs is the relationships that occur between married men in their early forties and single women in their twenties. James, in our earlier case illustration, is a good example of this common occurrence.

Married males experience an intense personal crisis in their early forties. Such men have a growing awareness of their own mortality. Often, a parent has recently died, and the middle-aged male sees younger men and women joining the labor force. He has worked hard for several years, sees death in the distance, and experiences an intense desire to be appreciated and to have fun. The man will not necessarily find appreciation at work because his supervisor and colleagues assume that he can do his job well. At home, his wife is no longer glowingly impressed, and his children are moving on in their own lives. His experience is one of time running out. What to do?

There is another group of persons in our culture, some of whom are also experiencing unmet emotional needs. These are women in their twenties who need to move away from home, to find a man who can protect and provide. They seek the excitement and glamour of the culture, and they long for affection and someone to look up to.

As with our example of James and Kate, it is not surprising that persons in each of these groups should link up for affairs. Their emotional needs at that point in time are compatible. But such individuals soon learn that affairs are hardly carefree. They increase the life stress of the parties involved with problems of time management, financial need, and the preoccupation with secrecy. More importantly, the emotional needs of each party are basic, intense, and not remedied by the sporadic encounters that characterize most affairs.

Now that we know that married people often have affairs to meet unfulfilled emotional needs, the question remains why so many of these needs are unmet in the first place. I believe the problem lies in our cultural overemphasis on excessive mastery.

Stress-resistant people have taught us that we need a reasonable balance between mastery and attachment for good health. We have also learned from John Bowlby (1969) that we are born with the need for caring attachments. Yet our culture drives us relentlessly to have it all, and as we have noted, most of us pursue excessive mastery and material gains, and neglect our caring attachments. We also correctly perceive that with everyone pursuing material goods, there actually are fewer caring attachments potentially present in our daily lives. Anxiety and sometimes panic set in as we reflect on the deficiencies in our attachments. We fear being abandoned in the midst of our material wealth. Pressed for time, we do not follow the steps that we have listed for making relationships work (trust, mutual respect, communication, shared economic responsibility, and time). We seek a quick answer. Since our culture has taught us (incorrectly) that love equals sex, in our haste and anxiety we may turn to the affair as the answer. We thus slip into the trap of defining our caring relationship with others as primarily sexual. This solution most often fails because the unmet needs are not primarily sexual. We all want to be loved, we all want caring attachments, but our advertising among other things has suggested the wrong solution. We all need to spend less time pursuing excessive material goods, and more time developing caring relationships. It is the pathway to greater stress resistance.

Stress-resistant individuals know this. When they face stressful life events, when their plans go awry, when their relationships fail, stress-resistant people often turn to caring for others, to sharing with others. They are aware that in time such efforts will keep their own problems in perspective.

Stress-resistant persons have an additional lesson to share with us about attachments. They realize that we live in a fast-paced, complex world filled with many people having many needs. They realize that none of us can have it all in terms of material goods, but they also know that none of us can have it all in terms of caring attachments either. They realize that there is not always enough human love to meet everyone's needs at any one time. They know that when we lack human love, when we feel abandoned, there are our philosophical and/or religious beliefs to support us. Recent medical research has demonstrated the power of such beliefs to reduce stress and maintain well-being. Individuals who believe in a Creator and Sustainer generally have better health. Religion and philosophy function in many ways. They can strengthen our human social contracts with supernatural sanctions; they can free us of unnecessary mastery when we have tried our best ("It is God's will now") as we have noted; and they can console us in adverse circumstances when our caring attachments fail us, fall apart, or end in death. It is beliefs such as these that facilitate adjustment in life's painful moments.

Life's traffic jams will be less a burden and our hearts will know some peace if we are able to develop caring attachments, and direct our energies towards loving others. Since there is so much con-fusion over what it means to love another person, we shall return to this issue in our last chapter. For the moment, let us focus our attention on the five fundamental building blocks necessary for caring human attachments that we have noted in this chapter.

9

MASTERY AND ATTACHMENT: THE SPECIAL PROBLEM OF LEARNED HELPLESSNESS

Character, like a photograph, develops in the darkness.
—Yosef Karsh

Rage, rage against the dying of the light.
—Dylan Thomas

Mr. Peterson was thirty-eight years old. He had always been quiet and hardworking. The local school principal, he was considered a good father and husband, and a community leader. Mrs. Peterson was thirty-five. She was thought of as quiet and hardworking. She was the receptionist at the local community hospital, and the mother of their only child, Maria.

Fourteen year old Maria, not surprisingly, was also quiet and hardworking. She had had good grades and was active in the school's chorus. She was also regularly and severely beaten by her alcoholic father.

It happened first when Maria was six. In bed for the night, she could not sleep because of the raging argument downstairs. Fearing someone would get hurt, little Maria ran to the kitchen to protect her mom. In red-faced fury, her father threw a steel frying pan, and hit Maria on the head. Blackness . . . Silence . . . No doctor was sent for.

It happened next at the dinner table. Dad was drunk. Maria was nervous. She sat as still as she could so that she would not cause

149

him to drink. Frightened, she kept eating like a good little soldier. Her hands trembled. She spilled some milk. . . .

Her father's deranged anger was followed by a pain in her shoulder unlike anything she had ever experienced. She found herself upside down, hurtling through the air, and landing on the bare flooring in the next room. She lay there whimpering like a wounded puppy that had been struck by a careless driver.

Her arm was reset by Dr. Ouellette at the local hospital where her mother worked. Her parents had explained that Maria had fallen off her bicycle. Dr. Ouellette sympathized with her parents' concern. He never asked Maria what had happened. She never volunteered. If your parents are supposed to protect you, what does a little girl do when the parents themselves are the source of danger? Her silent tears fell no more.

As the abuse continued and the years passed, Maria's grades failed, she left the school chorus, she was having nightly flashbacks of the violence. She managed to tolerate this family war zone by becoming psychologically numb. No feelings, no pain. It seemed like a possible compromise. She trusted no one, she had given up. She became chronically depressed.

What did it mean to love someone? Each night just before bedtime she knelt down, and asked her God, who did not answer, to send some young knight to rescue her from the darkness.

Maria is suffering from posttraumatic stress disorder (numbing phase) with learned helplessness. Her sense of mastery and caring attachments has been destroyed by her father's physical abuse exacerbated by his alcoholism, and by her mother's indifference. In her violent world, Maria made the (correct) assumption that she could not solve her father's problems. She then went to a second (and false) assumption that nothing could be done about anything.

Abraham Lincoln once said that defeat strikes the young the hardest because they least expect it. But this is true of older people also. All of us can be stunned by some event that renders us unable to respond for a period of time. Life is not fair, and, as bad as our circumstances may have seemed to us, others of us may have faced even more overwhelming and catastrophic events.

When an individual is confronted with an overwhelming life event that is potentially life threatening or that can have some extremely painful consequences, and from which there is no escape no matter how hard the individual tries, that person is confronted with psychological trauma. In the words of Tom Dooley, MD, the list, "of man's inhumanity to man," that can produce such trauma is lengthy: child and family physical abuse, sexual abuse, combat, street crime, terrorism, holocausts, motor vehicle accidents, political torture, parental alcoholism. To this list we need to add natural and inadvertent man-made disasters.

Each of these events can leave an individual in high stress after its occurrence, hence the name: posttraumatic stress disorder. Some individuals (like stress-resistant persons) seem to be able to use their sense of mastery and attachment to deal with the aftermath of the problem and to go on with life. Others are not so fortunate. They seem unable to bounce back. They remain helpless, their capacity to function is severely limited, and often they turn to drugs and alcohol to medicate their suffering.

How do these events so disrupt normal human functioning? What keeps some individuals from responding adequately? Were they ill-equipped to begin with or are certain events just too massive for the human mind to integrate? Can nothing be done for these persons who feel so helpless? Must they remain disengaged from the world around them until their deaths? Such questions form the substantive matter before us.

The Nature of Psychological Trauma

Psychological trauma is the state of severe fright we experience when we realize that a potentially life-threatening event with painful consequences has befallen us, and that no matter what we attempt, we are unable to respond effectively. Our resources have been overtaxed. Such an individual experiences anxiety, then panic, and then a dazed sense of bewilderment when the event is over.

Posttraumatic stress disorder (PTSD) frequently follows such episodes as these. It is characterized by two distinct phases: the acute or protest phase, and the chronic or numbing phase.

The Acute/Protest Phase. This phase usually occurs within the first six months of the event. It is characterized by anger and anxiety as the person deals with several different issues: mastery, attachments, changes in thinking, changes in body chemistry, and attempts to make some meaning of the event.

The victim seeks first to reestablish mastery. Legal proceedings, lawsuits, and insurance claims are victim attempts to restore mastery. Going over the event in one's mind or in reality to see what could have been done differently are also attempts at regaining mastery. During this period, the victim may lash out at "safe" others not involved in the event as the anger is displaced from the perpetrator to someone more neutral. These forums for expressing and channeling anger may help the victim to reassert some mastery over his or her environment.

During the protest phase, the victim also seeks to reestablish contact with others. Others with whom the victim has caring attachments can be helpful in reviewing the event, sharing the burden, reassuring the victim that others still care about him or her, and in gathering information on how to cope during the aftermath.

The protest phase is also characterized by changes in the victim's thinking where assumptions about the world are altered in at least three important ways (Janoff-Bulman, 1985). The victim's belief in personal invulnerability is shattered through the encounter with an unpredictable event over which he or she had no control. The belief that the world is comprehensible, predictable, and meaningful is no longer acceptable for the same reasons. Finally, the victim's view of him or herself as a competent adult worthy of self-esteem is shattered. In the face of this powerlessness, many victims blame themselves since it gives them the illusion of control. If they are at fault, the implication is that they can do something the next time to prevent the recurrence of the traumatic episode. All victims struggle to find meaning, to make sense of the event, to understand why it happened.

Last in the protest phase, the impact of the event is registered in the victim's body. He or she may experience an exaggerated startle response, hyperalertness, problems in concentrating, sleep disturbances, intrusive memories of the event, and flashbacks during sleep. The last three appear to be the core signs of PTSD (Lavelle and Mollica, 1985).

The Chronic/Numbing Phase. If the impact of the traumatic event is not treated during the acute phase (and much trauma is not), the victim enters the numbing phase.

Since the body cannot sustain a continued period of intense anxiety and rage forever, it resolves this issue by limiting its capacities to respond. The victim becomes less interested in doing things in the world, thinking is constricted, and feelings become very shallow or numb. Attempts at mastery and attachment have failed, the assumptive world remains shattered, the core PTSD symptoms remain, and the person becomes chronically depressed.

During the numbing phase, some victims have a tendency to repeat acts highly similar to the original traumatic event. A rape victim may become sexually promiscuous. A combat veteran may start a fight in a neighborhood bar. These reenactments happen, but it is not clear why they do.

One theory proposed that victims go through these events to regain mastery. A second theory has been offered by Dr. Bessel van der Kolk (1987) of Harvard Medical School. He noted that the rape victim, the battered spouse, the combat veteran often experience *relief* when they reenact their painful life event. He has suggested that, while our endorphins are generally shut off after a stressful life event, there appears to be one exception to this rule. If a person confronts a situation highly analogous to the original trauma, the victim's endorphins will come back on for one and a half hours, and the person will experience some relief for that time period. Victims may thus be engaging in repetitive behavior to self-medicate the aftermath of trauma. Should this explanation prove accurate, it would lead to improved ways of helping the victims of psychological trauma.

Learned Helplessness

For some unfortunate victims in the PTSD numbing phase, their response to the original trauma is further complicated by the problem of learned helplessness. These victims, in addition to having failed at restoring mastery and attachment, and regaining a more normal assumptive view of the world, compound this painful state of events by adding Maria's false assumption: They reason that, because they could do nothing about the original trauma, they can do nothing about other life events. They further assume that no one else can help them. They have learned to be helpless. It is very difficult to counsel such victims because they assume that the counselor can do nothing to aid them either. To help such victims, the counselor must resolve the learned helplessness first before the traumatic event itself can be addressed.

Seligman's Findings. Psychologist Martin Seligman (1975) has taught us much about the problem of learned helplessness. Between 1965 and 1969, Seligman and his colleagues placed dogs in harnesses so that they could not escape. Next, they applied electric shock to the animals' forepaws. No matter what it did, the animal could not escape the shock.

The animal was then placed in a large rectangular cage divided in half by a shoulder-high barrier. They had to jump over the barrier from one side of the cage to the other to avoid shock to their forepaws from the floor of the cage. This time, however, the situation was different. The animals could do something to solve their problem. What did Seligman's dogs do?

In two-thirds of his 150 animals, Seligman (1975) noticed several disruptions of normal canine routine. His animals made fewer attempts to jump the barrier, they became less mobile, and more passive. They lost their motivation, accepted the shocks, and withdrew into a corner of the cage. They looked "depressed." These findings were quite dissimilar to others of his dogs that had no previous experience with shock in the harness, and learned to jump the barrier quite easily. Seligman concluded that, when any organism (including humans) believes that its attempts to cope effectively to solve a problem will have no effect in solving that problem, the organism will stop trying. It will learn to be helpless.

Findings on Humans. While there have been attempts to explain the propensity to develop learned helplessness in humans as possibly resulting from a deficit at birth or as a form of a biological depressed state, Seligman's psychological theory has generated the most research on human beings, and remains our best understanding of this phenomenon at the moment.

Hundreds of studies on humans have been undertaken, and four basic characteristics of learned helplessness have emerged from this research.

The first characteristic relates to reasonable mastery. In learned helplessness, the individual does *not perceive* him or herself as having *any reasonable control or mastery*. They rely on others to solve their problems for them or they do not work at resolving their life stress at all. They allow life stress to overtake them by default.

The second characteristic is a *state of passivity*, or noninvolvement in the world around them. We saw this in Maria. After many years of abuse, she became uninterested in the world of a young teenager. She lost interest in school, sports, parties, and dates.

Persons with this passivity have no commitment to a task in life that is important to them. Nothing makes life really meaningful.

The third characteristic is *disrupted daily routines*. Persons with helplessness often have problems organizing a day. They may not eat regular meals, their sleep may become disturbed, and their sexual interest may be disrupted. In a rape victim with learned helplessness, for example, this individual might move every six months to minimize the chances of her assailant finding her again. Parents who are helpless often have great difficulty raising their children because they are overwhelmed by their own disrupted basic life-style routines.

Finally, helpless persons become *socially isolated*. They avoid other people, and deny themselves all of the potential benefits of caring human attachments that we have discussed. The nature of the painful events that have caused the helplessness has led the individual to trust no one. The avoidance of others precludes caring attachments.

While Seligman (1975) has basically understood helplessness as the loss of motivation arising from the false assumption that the individual has lost control and has become helpless and thus hopeless, recent medical evidence has suggested that helplessness may arise for other psychological reasons also, such as feelings of worthlessness, powerlessness, or even for adaptive survival in some very difficult situations. While further research will be needed to sort all of this out, the common end result of learned helplessness is the feeling of being *depressed*. This depression can last for years as it did in the case of Maria. Months, years, decades of people's lives can be spent in such an unhappy state. The toll from learned helplessness in terms of lost productivity and personal misery in people's lives is not insignificant.

Risk Factors. While any one of us can be confronted with the psychological trauma of an overwhelming life event, not everyone then goes on to develop PTSD or PTSD with learned helplessness. Medical research, including our own experience in the Victims of Violence Program at Cambridge Hospital, has delineated some of the risk factors that increase the probability of developing PTSD with helplessness after some catastrophic event.

The theme in this book has been that reasonable mastery and caring attachments are our major resources in coping with life stress. The theme is especially true in dealing with psychological trauma. If one's sense of mastery and/or one's network of caring attachments are weak, such an individual may be at higher risk for PTSD and helplessness because he or she is vulnerable to begin with.

A second risk factor is living in a dysfunctional family. In homes like Maria's where there is chaos due to substance abuse, major mental illness, or constant threats of divorce or violence, the opportunities to learn reasonable mastery and to be buffered from life stress by caring others are greatly diminished. Not every child growing up in such a home becomes an unhappy adult, but many do. For example, as many as half of all children with alcoholic parents may become alcoholics themselves as adults. Many of the others who remain abstinent marry alcoholics. Dysfunctional families increase risk.

Certain aspects of the traumatic event itself can increase risk as well. One traumatic episode is often easier to overcome than a series of traumas. Multiple traumas, such as those reported by battering and incest victims, increase the probability of PTSD and helplessness. The length of time involved is another important factor. When the single or multiple traumas occurred, did they happen in the course of a month or two, or did they happen over several years as in the case of Maria? The longer the person has been a victim, the greater the likelihood that serious psychological consequences will arise.

The person's developmental age at which the event took place is also a risk factor. As a general rule, the younger the person, the greater the probability of subsequent disturbance. For example, a victim of incest at age three is usually more vulnerable than an adult victim of a street mugging. Whether the victim knew the assailant or not makes a difference in trauma inflicted by humans. Crimes committed by a known assailant are often more devastating than pain inflicted by an unknown perpetrator. The known assailant usually is or has been part of the victim's network of caring attachments, and thus betrayal is added to the violence.

Another important risk factor is how the human family responds to the victim. We know that sharing or disclosing the event to another person can be a helpful first step in overcoming the effects of psychological trauma, if the caring other is supportive. If the victim cannot disclose the pain, as was the case with Maria, or if the victim discloses the event to a nonsupportive person, the risks of developing helplessness increase. There are many common examples of others not being supportive. I recently treated a patient who had been raped. Many years later she finally decided to tell her family. Her family legally disowned her when they heard of the rape. It is not at all rare that a teenage victim of childhood incest will finally tell the other parent of the abuse, only to find the nonperpetrating parent ordering the child to leave the home. By the very nature of their institutional procedures, well-intentioned police, prosecutors, and courts often end up, in effect, punishing the victim for disclosing the crimes. This happens through public testimony, cross-examination, and the like. Failures in disclosure usually increase the risk of subsequent psychological distress.

Finally, as human research findings have become available, Seligman himself has sought to refine his explanation about the onset of learned helplessness. He has noticed three cognitive factors that increase the probability that the person who fails to alter the outcome of the traumatic event will then go on to assume that he or she can then have no mastery over any other events in his or her life.

The first factor is the psychological need for personal control. As we have seen throughout this book, stress-resistant persons exercise some reasonable mastery. However, for the person who has need for excessive personal control, he or she is at higher risk of developing learned helplessness. Such persons hold themselves personally accountable for mastering situations that no one could reasonably expect to control. Such persons, for example, may hold themselves unnecessarily responsible for the anger of others, or the faulty driving of others, or the perpetual happiness of others. Such expectations of the self are too high.

The second cognitive factor is our perception of the painful event as being of short or long duration. Persons who view the traumatic event as one more instance of a long-standing pattern of negative events are more likely to develop helplessness.

The third cognitive factor has to do with the victim's understanding of the trauma as one specific event in which he or she lost control versus the assumption that this event was one in a long series of problems over which he or she has had no reasonable mastery. This overgeneralization from specific event to global (and defective) coping process increases the probability of the development of learned helplessness.

In summary, the more a person possesses the risk factors that we have noted, and the cognitive factors that Seligman has written about, the greater becomes the likelihood that he or she might develop PTSD with learned helplessness in the aftermath of coping with a catastrophic, potentially life-threatening event.

What can we do to correct this?

Seligman's Treatment Approach. As his understanding of the nature of learned helplessness increased, Seligman remained interested in possible ways of treating learned helplessness.

He began by shutting off the electric current to the grid floor of the dog cage, and by removing the shoulder-high barrier in its center. The cage was now safe, and his dogs were free to roam.

We might call his first approach the "time heals all wounds" theory. He placed the dogs back in the cage; they withdrew to the corner as they previously had. Seligman waited. He wanted to see if the animals would become curious, gradually reexamine the cage, and learn that it was safe. Seligman hoped that this might resolve the helplessness. The animals didn't budge—not even when they were hungry and were offered meat.

Not to be outdone, Seligman had a second approach. We might call this the "when you fall off of your bicycle, get up and immediately ride it again" theory. In medicine, this is known as in vivo desensitization. Basically, you take the person back to the scene of the accident or crime as soon as possible to demonstrate to the victim that the area is no longer unsafe (assuming that it is so).

For his part, Seligman decided to drag the animals across the grid floor to prove to them that it was safe. He dragged his dogs (some weighing as much as 150 pounds) back and forth across the cage. Although he had to drag some as many as two hundred times, eventually all of his animals had at least some partial recovery from their helplessness.

Forced reexposure was time-consuming (as well as tiring!), and was not always fully effective. In the subsequent twenty years, neither Seligman nor any other health care provider has offered an effective treatment for the problem of learned helplessness.

From Victim to Survivor: Project SMART

It is my belief that Seligman's research (1975) yielded a second important finding that has received no attention from the medical community nor from Seligman himself. Our attention has been so focused on learned helplessness that we have overlooked the fact that only two-thirds of Seligman's dogs became helpless. One-third of his animals did not feel trapped in the cage, did not refuse to jump the barrier, did not passively accept the shocks, or become helpless and "depressed." They remained resilient, "stress-resistant" if you will. I was struck by the paradox of learned helplessness in some and the resiliency in others.

As I thought more about the findings on human helplessness, it occurred to me that my stress-resistant persons were using the very strategies for coping that victims with learned helplessness did not appear to have. I have summarized these differences in table 1.

Stress-resistant persons have personal control, and are committed to and involved in tasks important to them. Helpless persons have no mastery, and are uninvolved in the world around them. Stress-resistant people have an adaptive and helpful life-style (few dietary stimulants/aerobic exercise/relaxation) where the helpless victim is beset with confusion. Stress-resistant people sought out caring attachments whereas those with learned helplessness avoided them. It seemed that people with learned helplessness and stress-resistant persons were at opposite ends of a continuum, a continuum ranging from poor coping to responding effectively to life stress.

Since the skills of stress-resistant persons by definition are effective in reducing stress, and enhancing mastery and attachment, I began to wonder if there might not be some way to teach these more effective skills to persons with learned helplessness. My goal

Table 1

Comparison of Coping Strategies:

LEARNED HELPLESSNESS	STRESS-RESISTANT PERSONS
1. No perceived control	1. Personal control
2. Passivity: No task involvement	2. Task involvement
3. Disruption of basic life-style	3. Adaptive life-style based on diet stimulant reduction/aerobic exercise/relaxation
4. Withdrawal from social support	4. Active seeking of social support
5. Mood: Depressed	5. Mood: Well-being

was to change the victim's expectations from no mastery to some mastery, from no caring attachments to some caring attachments. Knowing that patients with helplessness are difficult to help because they assume the clinician cannot do anything to solve life's problems, I was additionally hopeful that by resolving the learned helplessness the victim's energies would then be freed up to work as an ally with the therapist to attenuate the impact of the original trauma.

Project SMART has been my approach. As you know from chapter 6, Project SMART is the group treatment approach that helps persons to reduce the physiology of stress, and to learn the more effective skills of stress-resistant persons. The challenge now was to see if Project SMART could also reverse the psychology of defeat, known as learned helplessness. Toward that end, my colleagues and I at the Cambridge (Masschusetts) Hospital, a teaching hospital of Harvard Medical School, have conducted several Project SMART groups for trauma victims.

To date, treatment outcome information is available for sixty-eight persons in nine groups (Flannery, 1987b). The psychological forms of trauma suffered by these patients include rape, incest, domestic violence, and family alcoholism.

These early findings are promising. There were sharp reductions in the physiology of stress experienced by these adult men and women. The victims reported less muscle tension, less sleep disturbance, fewer outbursts of temper, and less generalized anxiety. These men and women also showed signs of enhanced mastery and the development of caring attachments. For example, victims reported taking more responsibility for household chores and child rearing, and becoming tactfully more assertive. Some patients also reported greater interpersonal cooperation, growing family cohesiveness, and the development of new friendships. Such were the signs of increased mastery and improved caring attachments.

Did this new psychology of mastery and attachment lead to a sound alliance with the therapist and to active attempts to resolve the trauma itself? The individual therapists for these patients report that this appears to be so. Many of these men and women returned to their individual counseling with a new sense of resolve to work hard in offsetting the negative impact that the various traumas have had on their lives.

The Project SMART approach to the treatment of learned helplessness is new. Its early results are encouraging, and we are hopeful that future research will more fully assess its suitability for this problem of helplessness. Should the early results be confirmed, Project SMART will be a powerful tool in reversing this psychology of defeat.

10

MASTERY, ATTACHMENT, AND MEANING: LOVE OF SELF AND OTHERS

Who's there?
—William Shakespeare, *Hamlet*

*You will always have happiness if you seek
and find how to serve.*
—Albert Schweitzer

Ellen mailed the check. She bit her tongue and fought back her tears of sadness. At the end of each month for nine years she had faithfully mailed this check. Even when she didn't have many dollars, she somehow always mailed this check. Now it was over. She held the photograph closely. Sorrow filled her heart.

Life was tough. This disease itself was hard enough, but the ridicule and rejection by others was the greater burden. Continuous rejection by others over a lifetime wore out one's spirit.

Things had begun normally enough. Her parents and brother were good people, family life was caring. She graduated from an excellent upper-middle-class suburban high school, and had enrolled in a top Ivy League college with plans for a career in law. She was twenty years old. Her parents had great hopes for her.

Then it happened. Suddenly. She started hearing voices that told her to harm herself; the television set seemed to speak to her with personal messages. She was terrified, very frightened of this strange experience, and suspicious of others. She had become insane.

The doctors had explained it to her clearly. She had a medical disease called schizophrenia. It was a medical disease just as arthritis or diabetes were medical diseases. From time to time, she was told, her schizophrenia would flare up just as these other two illnesses did. These flare-ups would affect her thinking rather than her joints or blood sugar, but with medicine she could lead a somewhat normal life.

That was nineteen years and several hospitalizations ago. At first, she could, in fact, work, but her disease became progressively more disabling. Repeated bouts with illness and poverty had worn out both her family and friends. Each episode brought more disorganization, more disability, more ridicule from strangers.

For the past nine years, however, Michael had always been there. Always loyal, always caring, he had never left her, and had always remembered to write each month. In his own way, he had helped her to go on, and she loved him dearly.

But now it had come to this. Her illness had become so disabling that she had to give up her part-time, minimum-wage job, and enter a nursing home at age forty-nine. Her funds, always limited, were now no more. Today's check would be the last. She could no longer hold back her tears. She anguished over what would happen to Michael, her Michael, her "adopted" nine-year-old brother in Brazil whom she had never met. Who would be his sponsor now?

In my years of practice, this was one of the most moving counseling sessions I have ever been present at. This woman with a severe medical illness, in complete poverty, and with head held high, has important lessons to teach all of us about caring and loving others. She maintained a meaningful purpose in life, even in the face of great pain and suffering.

We live in an age characterized by much interpersonal harshness. People are often rude, or even physically and/or verbally abusive. They steal, they maim, and commit many other types of heinous acts against others. While it is true that such behavior has always been with us, the present experience of many is that such violence and inconsiderateness now reaches into their own neighborhoods where they previously felt safe and sheltered from the world's many wars.

Yet here is an unknown woman who has much to teach us about good self-esteem and its power in enabling us to love others, even in such often harsh times as our own. As Nietzsche wrote: A person who has a *why* to live for can bear almost any *how*. In an age of material saturation and surfeit, loving others may be the *why* that many are seeking—a purposeful meaning in life.

As Ellen understood, we cannot love others unless we love ourselves. The "self" is central in managing stress effectively for it is involved in the strongest of human emotions: love, hatred, jealousy, loneliness. We shall look at each of these emotions in turn after we have reviewed the development of the self, the self that links us to others.

The Self

The Development of the Self. Our self is our awareness (conscious and unconscious) of our mind and our body as they interact with the physical environment around us and the members of the human family present to us at any point in history. It is our awareness of our personhood, our uniqueness, and our core being. The founding fathers of our country understood its importance, and granted to each "self" in law-bound volumes certain inalienable rights. If we believe and value our "self," we will be better able to cope with life stress, to attain better stress resistance. If we continually regard our selves as bad, defective, or damaged goods, we will pay a great price in ill health and human misery.

Our self-evaluation process includes three components: life events, evaluations of each event, and a general inference from those specific evaluations about our overall functioning as a person.

As events occur in our lives, we evaluate how well or poorly we responded to them. Let us consider Tom, a shoe salesman, as he deals with some common life events. The first is driving to work, which he does safely and on time. He correctly evaluates himself as having done that task well. His remaining events are interactions with his customers during the day. He sells five customers pairs of shoes, two customers refuse to buy from his store, and one is angry with Tom personally for defective shoes from the factory. Tom gives some thought to how he could have improved his salesmanship with the two customers who did not make a purchase, and he loses his composure with the irate customer.

Tom will now do what each of us should do. He will review the nine events, and see that he mastered six and needed to improve on three. From these specific evaluations, he is now able to make a general inference about his "self." He concludes that, on balance, he is a responsible employee and a good salesperson.

This is the normal process for "self" evaluation: Responding to specific events, making specific evaluations of each, and then making a general inference about the self from all of the specific evaluations. The norms we employ in this evaluation process are the values and moral standards of the culture. If we follow this process, take stock of our functioning regularly, remain consistent with our culture's higher values, evaluate feedback from others, and try to improve where we can, we will be able to make adequate and accurate statements about our self-competence and worth. Our self-esteem will be developing adequately, and we will feel good about ourselves.

There are at least three ways in which the normal development of the self and adequate self-esteem can be impeded. The first is by blatant disregard of society's moral and legal values. Sociopaths and narcissists often flaunt society's normative standards. Their interaction with others often ends in poor outcomes because of this, and they are usually quickly avoided by others.

A second possible pathway to inadequate development of the self happens in men and women who do not take the time to evaluate specific events as they go along, and/or who additionally fail to evaluate feedback from others. Such persons usually make a general inference about their behavior at some point. Such global statements are often incorrect because memory is a frail tool and sometimes inaccurate. The end result is a person who does not truly know his or her strengths and weaknesses.

A third possible route to poor self-esteem is continuous faulty negative thinking. Medical researchers Aaron Beck (1970) and Albert Ellis (1963) have taught us about this tendency always to see one's self in a poor light even when there is no factual reason to do so. For those persons who tend to be highly self-critical, frustration and depression frequently follow.

Dr. Beck has focused his attention on faulty thinking strategies. These include overgeneralizing from one event to all events ("Because this didn't go smoothly, nothing will go right"); discounting the positive ("Yes, I did that correctly; but I did these other two things wrong"); magnifying one's imperfections ("Sure, I got all

A's, but I was too small for the football team"); and an all-or-nothing mind-set ("If this evening doesn't go right, I'll never date again").

Dr. Ellis has studied faulty, overbearing assumptions that some persons make as part of their self-evaluative process. Some of the more common include statements like: "I am a worthless person when I act foolishly or badly"; "I am a bad and unlovable person when I am rejected"; "People *must* treat me fairly"; "It is horrible when major things don't go my way."

If you are an inconsistent or negative self-evaluator, you are increasing your life stress unnecessarily. Take the time to evaluate your responses to specific events on their own merits as you go along. In this way, you can be assured that your general inference about your "self" will be most accurate. You have strengths and weaknesses like all of us. Both need to be understood and integrated.

Stages of Growth for the Self. As we proceed through life, there are certain tasks involved in growth that each of us encounters. These are normal, predictable stages of adulthood. How we resolve these tasks of growing and maturing ultimately is added to or detracted from our sense of self esteem. Several distinguished scholars (Erikson, 1963; Hennig and Jardin, 1977; Levinson, 1978; Vaillant, 1977) have studied human development. The following discussion summarizes what they have learned:

In the decade of our *twenties,* our major tasks are to clarify our basic values, to find employment (mastery) so that we can become a contributing member of society, and to begin to develop intimacy (attachments) with others. This process is delayed by some years if we have spent time studying in professional or graduate schools. Our *thirties* are a period of developing in more detail our initial life goals. Marriage, children, housing, or some community project are all ways of becoming rooted in our plans. Our early *forties* are characterized by intense turmoil as we saw in James in the case illustration of chapter 8. Often initiated by the death of a parent, we sense our own mortality, and reevaluate what we have accomplished to this point in our lives. Do we still believe in the same basic values? Are we satisfied with our careers, our marriages, our children, our investments? Often major changes are made in our lives if we are dissatisfied with our first answers. Time is running out.

The decades of the *fifties* and *sixties* are usually marked by being generative and concerned with the development of others. At these ages, we will act as mentors for younger people at work, spend time with our grandchildren, or perhaps become involved in some community project. Our later years leave us with our retirement dreams, but also with the last stages of personal growth: coping with aging, physical degeneration, and death. We struggle to find a meaning for our lives by integrating what we have done well and not so well, and by leaving some form of legacy, a marker by which the human family will remember us. For some, this is through children; for others this is through one's life work, the arts, acts of charity, or by some other individual means of generativity.

As we move through these various life stages, we will learn of our strengths as well as of the areas where we need improvement. By self-reflection and feedback from others, our sense of self will emerge. Good self-esteem is not to be equated with status or material possessions. All of these can be taken from us. Rather, good self-esteem is a product of reasonable mastery and caring attachments. If we have responded to the life stress each of us must face by adhering to the basic value standards of our culture when we have resolved these problems, then we can take satisfaction in who we are. We will have good self-esteem, and the foundations for healthy self-love. This love of self with its core strengths can then be directed toward the welfare of others, in particular toward loving others, the highest form of caring attachments.

If we discount our strengths, however, and ignore our weaknesses and the cultural moral code, our self-esteem will be poor. Our capacity for self-love will be greatly diminished, our ability to relate effectively to others will be curtailed, and we will place ourselves at potential risk for lives marred by hatred, jealousy, envy, and loneliness. We shall look at each of these powerful human emotions in turn.

The Other

Love. Love is sex, love is power, love is possessions, love is status, love is primarily a state of feelings. Such are the messages in our culture, and so it should not surprise us that we are often confused about what love really is.

What does it mean to love another person? Love is helping another person grow to his or her potential without expecting anything in return, provided that neither party is being physically or verbally abused. The experience of such love is a sense of contentment or inner peace for the helping person. It is this understanding that is the philosophical bedrock for developing stress resistance. Loving others creates perspective, and a purposeful meaning in life.

There are three parts to this definition. The first is fairly clear. Love is a willful act of involvement with another to help the other person grow to his or her potential. The person who would love needs to consider the assets and liabilities of the other, and then determine how best to help the other reach his or her potential. Sometimes it is by teaching mastery, at other times by providing caring attachment and listening, and at still other times by setting limits on the other who may be setting forth on a path that is not in his or her best interests. This task requires hard work and self-discipline on the part of the person who would love. While we continue to lead our own lives, we cannot let our goals dictate the direction of the other. Such a process requires continuous thought and attention.

The second part of our definition requires that we seek nothing for ourselves in return. This may be particularly difficult in our age of self-gratification, but it is an important aspect of loving. We cannot expect the other to help us when we are in difficulty, we cannot expect the other to love or even like us, we cannot expect even to feel good for having helped out. When we offer our love to the other, there can be no hidden agendas, no strings attached, no hesitations. It is true it would be pleasant if there was reciprocity and feelings of goodwill, but this does not always occur. We can expect nothing from the other.

The third part of the definition is of equal importance to the first two: *neither* party is being abused. We all may inadvertently offend each other on occasion, but I am referring here to relationships in which one or both parties are continually exposed to physical or verbal abuse. You cannot love another well no matter how admirable your intent, if you are the focus of attack or if you are expected to give up your own needs completely for the other. We must also love ourselves and not let our own potential be destroyed. In such circumstances, the most caring thing we may be able to do is to leave the relationship because our presence enables the other to continue the abuse and to destroy his or her own self. True love, on the other hand, should lead to the other person's having increased self-esteem.

People sometimes feel guilty when they do not like their parents or their own children. It is helpful to understand the difference between moral guilt and psychological guilt. When we transgress the rules of God or man as expressed in society's laws, we are morally guilty. We have deliberately violated some code. Psychological guilt arises when we are attempting to meet some superhuman expectation that we have of ourselves or that someone else is imposing on us. If, for example, you as a parent have done for your children what society reasonably expects, but you do not like your eldest child's drug abuse and want to have less to do with him or her, and consequently feel guilty about it, you are experiencing psychological guilt. Since you have done nothing to violate moral codes, it is not an issue of moral guilt. Either you are expecting too much of yourself as a parent, or your offspring's demands upon you are too great. Such psychological guilt can be resolved by assessing the realistic expectations in specific circumstances.

After completing ten volumes of the history of civilization, after studying the human family over these many centuries, Will Durant (Durant and Durant, 1968) was asked for his observation on what had been the best way to cope with stress throughout all of human history. His observation and suggestion was to love everyone and eventually you will get along.

Evil. Human-induced evil is the deliberate, conscious attempt to destroy the potential for life and growth in another. The planned goal of harming someone else can be either physical or psychological. The experience of evil can be seen in extreme rage or hatred, jealousy or envy, or the desire for revenge (See Peck, 1983).

Just as the ability to love others flows from high self-esteem, destructive rage begins in part in individuals with poor self-esteem. Such men and women often feel powerless and without mastery or are extremely dependent. They sometimes use the hatred/rage to destroy a relationship and often to inflict harm on another. Jealousy and envy are often found in such persons. These latter two states are frequently marked by anger and often by hatred.

Jealousy is most easily understood as intense anger because the jealous person is fearful that the other will take something that he or she has and feels powerless to protect. Envy is somewhat analogous. In envy, the envious person wants something that the other has and which the envious person feels unable to attain by his or her own efforts.

From the perspective of stress resistance, such rageful anger and deliberate harm of others is not adaptive. They create life stress, tax coping resources, waste time, alienate others, and keep the stress response in overdrive with the end result of impaired functioning.

Loneliness. Loneliness is the absence of caring attachments and the meaning in life that such attachments bring us. Many life events can lead to loneliness: our dreams fail, we move away from loved ones, we become divorced, we get promoted and must leave our colleagues behind. (See Peplau and Pearlman, 1982, for a more detailed discussion.)

All of us experience loneliness in our lives because we often have no control over what precipitates our separation from others. However, we do have some control over what maintains our loneliness once it has started. Much of chronic loneliness stems from poor self-esteem, and may include fear of rejection, fear of dependency, or trying to attain excessively high standards set by others.

The sadness and depression we experience in loneliness is nature's way of teaching us how important we are to each other. When loneliness befalls us, we need to address it directly by being active in the world around us, by avoiding negative thinking (e.g. "I can't go on without her"), and by helping and loving others as stress-resistant people do. We need to force ourselves to do this even when it is the last thing in the world we want to do. Activity mitigates depressive feelings and loneliness, and leads to new relationships with others.

If you grew up in a dysfunctional family, your fear of rejection may greatly inhibit you from beginning to be with others. You were lonely as a child, and you may remain isolated as an adult. You deserve better. Seek some professional counseling.

Keeping Life in Perspective: The Self and the Other

As we near the end of our journey in learning how to develop stress resistance, we want to spend a few moments on the importance of attaining a perspective on life. To see events properly in the larger frame of one's lifetime and in the history of the human family can be very helpful in enhancing our self-esteem, our capacity for stress resistance, and our resolve in dealing with life's traffic jams.

Aaron Antonovsky (1979, 1987) refers to this perspective as one's sense of coherence. He defines this sense of coherence as having three parts. First, it must provide our lives with meaning, a belief that life's tasks are worthy of our involvement. Second, it must offer us a sense of comprehensibility, the capacity to understand and reasonably predict events in life. Lastly, it must provide us with a sense of manageability, a reasonable expectation that we can influence life's events to ensure the outcomes we seek. Others express a similar concept when they speak of their personal values, their ethical or religious code, or their personal philosophy of life. We can look to nature, history, philosophy, and religion for experiences and values that can help us attain this sense of perspective and meaning.

In our natural world, the tide goes in and out about every twelve hours. The earth circles the sun every three-hundred-and-sixty-five days, and each of these has been happening regularly for millions of years. Does any of us need more than three meals a day? Can we wear more than one set of clothes at a time? What is the rush? History indicates that only a handful of individuals in any generation have any meaningful impact a generation later. What are the probabilities of any of us being in that small group? The body is not built to rush constantly. Is it worth your health and happiness? In the meantime, one-third of the world will go to bed hungry tonight. Many others will die never having known freedom in their entire lives. Are we appreciative of what we have? The messages from nature to help us keep things in perspective are everywhere. We need only look.

History can also be helpful to us. History can help us understand the origins and purposes of human life. It provides moral examples and a meaning for living both to individuals and to nations. History also presents solutions to many of the basic and recurring human life problems over the centuries (Plumb, 1970). For example, life's traffic jams have been mentioned at times in this book, both in the concrete and in metaphor. Yet traffic jams are not new. The streets of ancient Rome were as badly congested as our own. At times, the Romans must have felt that all of life was surely a traffic jam, but cope they did, and they left us notes on how to do it. Santayana has noted that those who do not examine the past are doomed to repeat it. This is a serious problem in our culture where many people do not read history even once. History provides us with many answers for coping with life stress, how to live for others, and how to bear the stress with grace when there is nothing that can be done.

For its part, philosophy helps us to cope with life stress by focusing our attention on the most basic questions in life. What is man? What is God? What is the meaning of life? What is the meaning of suffering and death? How am I related to the other members of the human family? The focus on these basic questions keeps us from magnifying the petty annoyances of daily life stress.

Religion with its similar focus on the ultimate questions in life can also enhance our sense of perspective. The great religions of the world encourage us to love others, to be generative toward others. It provides us with a way of understanding events beyond our control. It enables us to cope with the pain and suffering and death that are part of being human by providing a transcendent meaning for such suffering.

Let me close with what my clients have taught me about perspective in two decades of counseling:

1. Life is short.
2. Change is constant.
3. Life is competitive.
4. Everything in moderation.
5. We have free choice.
6. Accept what we cannot change.
7. Love one another.

These are basic lessons that the human family has known for as long as humans have faced life stress and life's traffic jams. These lessons have provided a sense of perspective and a meaningful purpose in life for those becoming stress resistant for generations. We have no reason to believe them to be any less true for our own age.

Becoming Stress-Resistant: A Final Word

We have covered a good many aspects of stress and a wide array of possible interventions to cope with it. Each of us now needs to develop our own plan for becoming stress-resistant, a plan tailored to our own personal circumstances and to the specific stressful life events that each of us faces.

In developing such plans, we need to list our goals and the various strategies we would like to implement over time to reach these objectives. We want to remember to do this in the small manageable steps that we have spoken of. We should start with something that we are really motivated to change, and something that we can, in fact, implement and master without great difficulty. When we have mastered this intervention, we should proceed to the next one, and so forth until we have completed our list of stress-resistant goals. We need to be mindful that some of these changes may take two years or longer. We can not rush our coping with stress, but, as we introduce these gradual changes, we should also feel increasingly well.

In choosing any one specific intervention, we want to keep in mind the basic characteristics of stress-resistance: (1) reasonable mastery; (2) sound health-maintenance practices including a balanced diet, aerobic exercise, and relaxation; (3) caring attachments to others; and (4) a basic concern for the welfare of others.

The following general guidelines may be of help as we begin our own personal programs:

1. None of us can have it all. It is helpful to bear this assumption in mind as we make what choices we wish.
2. Employ a right-brain stress reduction activity early on. As we have seen such activities help us to reduce our stress fairly quickly, and they enhance our capacity to reason out our choices clearly because such activities improve concentration.
3. Develop the reasonable mastery skills of stress-resistant persons. Use Project *SMART* as a beginning step.
4. Develop the attachment skills of stress-resistant persons.
5. Love one another. It helps us keep things in perspective and provides a purposeful meaning in life.

It is my hope that each of you will become more stress-resistant, and enjoy the health and sense of well-being that can be yours.

We Needn't Lose Sleep Unnecessarily over Life's Stress.

"I find you up in the middle of the winter and you tell me nothing's wrong?"

Appendix A: Your Stress-Resistance: Self-Assessment Questionnaires

Here are some self-assessment questionnaires that measure life stress, mastery, and human attachments. These questionnaires do not have the medical precision of laboratory tests or CAT scans, but they can be helpful guides for us. If you wish, complete these questionnaires.

Questionnaire 1

Indicate those changes listed below that have occurred in your life in the last twelve months by circling the number after the event.

Death of spouse	100	Business readjustment	39
Divorce	73	Change in financial state	38
Marital separation	65	Death of a close friend	37
Detention in jail	63	Change to a different line of work	36
Death of a close family member	63	Change in number of arguments with spouse	35
Personal injury or illness	53	Mortgage or loan greater than $10,000	31
Marriage	50	
Being fired from work	47	Foreclosure of mortgage or loan	30
Retirement from work	45	
Marital reconciliation	45	Change in responsibilities at work	29
Change in health or behavior of family member	44	Son or daughter leaving home	29
Pregnancy	40	In-law troubles	29
Sexual difficulties	39	Outstanding personal achievement	28
Gain of new family member	39	

Wife beginning or ceasing work	26	Change in recreational habits	19
Beginning or ceasing formal school	26	Change in Church activities	19
Change in living conditions	25	Mortgage or loan less than $10,000	17
Revision of personal habits	24	Change in social activities	18
Troubles with the boss	23	Change in sleeping habits	16
Change in residence	20	Change in eating habits	15
Change in working hours or conditions/ responsibilities	20	Change in number of family get-togethers	15
		Vacation	13
Change in schools	20	Christmas	12
		Minor violations of the law	11

Questionnaire 2

Directions: Hassles are irritants that can range from minor annoyances to fairly major pressures, problems or difficulties. They can occur few or many times.

Listed on the following pages are a number of ways in which a person can feel hassled. First, circle the hassles that have happened to you *in the past month*. Then look at the numbers on the right of the items you circled. Indicate by circling a 1, 2, or 3 how SEVERE each of the circled hassles has been for you in the past month. If a hassle did not occur in the last month, do NOT circle it.

SEVERITY
1. Somewhat severe
2. Moderately severe
3. Extremely severe

HASSLES

(1) Misplacing or losing things	1	2	3
(2) Troublesome neighbors	1	2	3
(3) Social obligations	1	2	3
(4) Inconsiderate smokers	1	2	3
(5) Troubling thoughts about your future	1	2	3
(6) Thoughts about death	1	2	3
(7) Health of a family member	1	2	3
(8) Not enough money for clothing	1	2	3
(9) Not enough money for housing	1	2	3
(10) Concerns about owing money	1	2	3
(11) Concerns about getting credit	1	2	3
(12) Concerns about money for emergencies	1	2	3
(13) Someone owes you money	1	2	3
(14) Financial responsibility for someone who doesn't live with you	1	2	3
(15) Cutting down on electricity, water, etc.	1	2	3
(16) Smoking too much	1	2	3
(17) Use of alcohol	1	2	3
(18) Personal use of drugs	1	2	3
(19) Too many responsibilities	1	2	3
(20) Decisions about having children	1	2	3
(21) Nonfamily members living in your house	1	2	3
(22) Care for pet	1	2	3
(23) Planning meals	1	2	3
(24) Concerned about the meaning of life	1	2	3
(25) Trouble relaxing	1	2	3
(26) Trouble making decisions	1	2	3
(27) Problems getting along with fellow workers	1	2	3

(28) Customers or clients who give you a hard time	1	2	3
(29) Home maintenance (inside)	1	2	3
(30) Concerns about job security	1	2	3
(31) Concerns about retirement	1	2	3
(32) Laid off or out of work	1	2	3
(33) Don't like current work duties	1	2	3
(34) Don't like fellow workers	1	2	3
(35) Not enough money for basic necessities	1	2	3
(36) Not enough money for food	1	2	3
(37) Too many interruptions	1	2	3
(38) Unexpected company	1	2	3
(39) Too much time on hands	1	2	3
(40) Having to wait	1	2	3
(41) Concerns about accidents	1	2	3
(42) Being lonely	1	2	3
(43) Not enough money for health care	1	2	3
(44) Fear of confrontation	1	2	3
(45) Financial security	1	2	3
(46) Silly practical mistakes	1	2	3
(47) Inability to express yourself	1	2	3
(48) Physical illness	1	2	3
(49) Side effects of medication	1	2	3
(50) Concerns about medical treatment	1	2	3
(51) Physical appearance	1	2	3
(52) Fear of rejection	1	2	3
(53) Difficulties with getting pregnant	1	2	3
(54) Sexual problems that result from physical problems	1	2	3
(55) Sexual problems other than those resulting from physical problems	1	2	3
(56) Concerns about health in general	1	2	3
(57) Not seeing enough people	1	2	3
(58) Friends or relatives too far away	1	2	3
(59) Preparing meals	1	2	3
(60) Wasting time	1	2	3
(61) Auto maintenance	1	2	3
(62) Filling out forms	1	2	3
(63) Neighborhood deterioration	1	2	3
(64) Financing children's education	1	2	3
(65) Problems with employees	1	2	3
(66) Problems on job due to being a woman or man	1	2	3

(67) Declining physical abilities	1	2	3
(68) Being exploited	1	2	3
(69) Concerns about bodily functions	1	2	3
(70) Rising prices of common goods	1	2	3
(71) Not getting enough rest	1	2	3
(72) Not getting enough sleep	1	2	3
(73) Problems with aging parents	1	2	3
(74) Problems with your children	1	2	3
(75) Problems with persons younger than yourself	1	2	3
(76) Problems with your lover	1	2	3
(77) Difficulties seeing or hearing	1	2	3
(78) Overloaded with family responsibilities	1	2	3
(79) Too many things to do	1	2	3
(80) Unchallenging work	1	2	3
(81) Concerns about meeting high standards	1	2	3
(82) Financial dealings with friends or acquaintances	1	2	3
(83) Job dissatisfactions	1	2	3
(84) Worries about decisions to change jobs	1	2	3
(85) Trouble with reading, writing, or spelling abilities	1	2	3
(86) Too many meetings	1	2	3
(87) Problems with divorce or separation	1	2	3
(88) Trouble with arithmetic skills	1	2	3
(89) Gossip	1	2	3
(90) Legal problems	1	2	3
(91) Concerns about weight	1	2	3
(92) Not enough time to do the things you need to do	1	2	3
(93) Television	1	2	3
(94) Not enough personal energy	1	2	3
(95) Concerns about inner conflicts	1	2	3
(96) Feel conflicted over what to do	1	2	3
(97) Regrets over past decisions	1	2	3
(98) Menstrual (period) problems	1	2	3
(99) The weather	1	2	3
(100) Nightmares	1	2	3
(101) Concerns about getting ahead	1	2	3
(102) Hassles from boss or supervisor	1	2	3
(103) Difficulties with friends	1	2	3

(104) Not enough time for family	1	2	3
(105) Transportation problems	1	2	3
(106) Not enough money for transportation	1	2	3
(107) Not enough money for entertainment and recreation	1	2	3
(108) Shopping	1	2	3
(109) Prejudice and discrimination from others	1	2	3
(110) Property, investments or taxes	1	2	3
(111) Not enough time for entertainment and recreation	1	2	3
(112) Yardwork or outside home maintenance	1	2	3
(113) Concerns about news events	1	2	3
(114) Noise	1	2	3
(115) Crime	1	2	3
(116) Traffic	1	2	3
(117) Pollution	1	2	3

HAVE WE MISSED ANY OF YOUR HASSLES? IF SO, WRITE THEM IN BELOW:

(118) _____   1   2   3

ONE MORE THING: HAS THERE BEEN A CHANGE IN YOUR LIFE THAT AFFECTED HOW YOU ANSWERED THIS SCALE? IF SO, TELL US WHAT IT WAS:

_____

Questionnaire 3

This questionnaire measures the different ways people respond to various situations in life. Select the one statement in each pair that is the most accurate for you. There are no right or wrong answers.

I more strongly believe that:	OR
Promotions are earned through hard work and persistence.	Making a lot of money is largely a matter of getting the right breaks.
In my experience I have noticed that there is usually a direct connection between how hard I study and the grades I get.	Many times the reactions of teachers seem haphazard to me.

The number of divorces indicates that more and more people are not trying to make their marriages work.	Marriage is largely a gamble.
When I am right I can convince others.	It is silly to think that one can really change another person's basic attitudes.
In our society, a man's future earning power is dependent upon his ability.	Getting promoted is really a matter of being a little luckier than the next guy.
If one knows how to deal with people they are really quite easily led.	I have little influence over the way other people behave.
In my case the grades I make are the results of my own efforts; luck has little or nothing to do with it.	Sometimes I feel that I have little to do with the grades I get.
People like me can change the course of world affairs if we make ourselves heard.	It is only wishful thinking to believe that one can really influence what happens in society at large.
I am the master of my fate.	A great deal that happens to me is probably a matter of chance.
Getting along with people is a skill that must be practiced.	It is almost impossible to figure out how to please some people.

Questionnaire 4

Instructions: We would like you to think about the people you feel close to and the people you feel you can depend upon for help, advice, companionship, etc. These people might be family members, other relatives, coworkers, friends, neighbors, clergy, etc.

Below are thirty True/False statements that deal with the types of things people feel they can ask of their friends, and the types of relationships people might have with one another.

For each statement, circle a *T* if the statement is *true* or *mostly true* for you; or circle an *F* if the statement is *false* or *mostly false* for you.

1. There is at least one person I know whose advice I really trust.   T   F

2. If I decide on a Friday afternoon that I would like to go to a movie that evening, I could find someone to go with me.   T   F

3. If for some reason I were put in jail, there is someone I could call on who would bail me out.   T   F

4. There is someone who will give me suggestions about activities for recreation or entertainment.   T   F

5. No one I know would throw a birthday party for me.   T   F

6. If I had to go out of town for a few weeks, someone I know would look after my house (the plants, pets, yard, etc.).   T   F

7. There is really no one who can give me objective feedback about how I'm handling my problems.   T   F

8. There are several different people with whom I enjoy spending time.   T   F

9. If I were sick and needed someone to drive me to the doctor, I would have trouble finding someone.   T   F

10. When I need suggestions for how to deal with a personal problem, I know someone to turn to.   T   F

11. I don't often get invited to do things with others.   T   F

12. There is no one I could call on if I needed to borrow a car for a few hours.   T   F

13. There is really no one who I feel comfortable going to for advice about sexual problems.   T   F

14. If I wanted to have lunch with someone, I could easily find someone to join me.   T   F

15. If I needed a quick emergency loan for $100, there is someone I could get it from.   T   F

16. There is someone I can turn to for advice about handling hassles over household responsibilities.   T   F

17. Most people I know don't enjoy the same   T   F
    things that I do.
18. If I needed some help in moving to a new   T   F
    home, I would have a hard time finding
    someone to help me.
19. I feel that there is no one with whom I   T   F
    can share my most private worries and
    fears.
20. When I feel lonely, there are several   T   F
    people I could call and talk to.
21. If I were sick, there would be almost no   T   F
    one I could find to help me with my daily
    chores.
22. If a family crisis arose, few of my friends   T   F
    would be able to give me good advice
    about handling it.
23. I regularly meet or talk with members of   T   F
    my family or friends.
24. If I got stranded 10 miles out of town,   T   F
    there is someone I could call to come get
    me.
25. There are very few people I trust to help   T   F
    solve my problems.
26. I feel that I'm on the fringe in my circle of   T   F
    friends.
27. If I had to mail an important letter at the   T   F
    post office by 5:00 and couldn't make it,
    there is someone who could do it for me.
28. There is someone I could turn to for   T   F
    advice about changing my job or finding
    a new one.
29. If I wanted to go out of town (e.g., to the   T   F
    coast) for the day, I would have a hard
    time finding someone to go with me.
30. If I needed a ride to the airport very early   T   F
    in the morning, I would have a hard time
    finding anyone to take me.

Scoring and Interpretation of Questionnaires

Now score and interpret your questionnaires with the instructions found below. Write in your answers in table 1, the health summary profile sheet, found on page 189.

1) Questionnaire #1—*The Social Readjustment Rating Scale* (Holmes & Rahe, 1967)

Scoring

This scale measures major life events which are the fundamental, if infrequent, disruptions in our lives that can lead to life stress.

Add together the numerical weights for each of the items that you have circled for a total sum score.

Interpretation

If your score is 150–199, you have a 37 percent chance of a minor illness in the next two years, if you do not do something more adaptive in managing your stress.

If your score is between 200–299, you have a 51 percent chance of developing a minor illness in the next two years, if you do nothing more adaptive to cope.

If your score is over 300, you have a 79 percent chance of a major health breakdown within the next two years. You may want to begin adding more effective strategies to help you cope with life stress.

---

2) Questionnaire #2—*The Daily Hassles Scale* (Kanner et al., 1981)

Scoring

Hassles are small daily events that taken together can increase life stress.

Add together all of the items that you have circled regardless of how severe you rated any item.

Interpretation

Most of us have about twenty-five or thirty hassles. If your score is greater than this, you have more than average stress from the small frustrating events of daily life, and a greater risk for stress-related illness.

---

3) Questionnaire #3—*Internal Control—External Control: A Sampler* (Rotter, 1971)

Scoring

Reasonable mastery or personal control is the amount of influence that we believe we have to shape events in our daily lives in ways that we would like.

Add up the items you have checked in the lefthand column for a total score. Add up the items you have checked in the righthand column for a total score. Your score in the lefthand column measures how much direct personal control to shape events you believe you have. Your score in the righthand column reflects how much influence to directly shape events that you do *not* believe you have.

Interpretation

Higher scores in the left hand column indicate you are inclined towards reasonable mastery or personal control. Reasonable mastery usually results in less stress-related illness.

---

4) Questionnaire #4—*The Social Support Index* (Revised) (Wilcox, 1981)

Scoring

This instrument measures how we utilize the caring attachments in our lives, and by inference how many networks we are embedded in. There are three subscales that measure the helpful types of interchanges outlined in chapter 4: Belonging (companionship), Tangible Support, and Emotional Support. Add the number of statements that you agree with for each subscale, and then add each of the three subscale scores together for a total score.

Belonging Subscale	*Tangible Subscale*	*Emotional Subscale*
2-T	3-T	1-T
5-F	6-T	4-T
8-T	9-F	7-F
11-T	12-F	10-T
14-T	15-T	13-F
17-F	18-F	16-T
20-T	21-F	19-F
23-T	24-T	22-F
26-T	27-T	25-F
29-T	30-F	28-F

Interpretation

The higher your subscale and total scores, the greater the strength of your caring attachments. Caring attachments usually result in fewer stress-related illnesses.

Your Health Profile Summary Sheet

As you survey your health profile sheet, you should have a better sense of the life stress confronting you, and the resources you have available to cope with such problems. Your scores may suggest some areas in which you wish to further develop your capacity for stress resistance.

Biological limitations speak for themselves. Any limitations you have from birth or have acquired in subsequent injuries in some way increases the effort you must put forth to solve the problems of life.

Life stress is determined by the amount of chronic illnesses you have (since they also complicate resolving life stress), plus the major life events and daily hassles you are required to cope with.

Your coping resources (reasonable mastery) and your social supports (caring attachments) are your resources for stress resistance.

I realize this exercise has been something like filling out your tax forms, but, if you have been able to follow along, you should now have a better sense of how similar you are to a stress-resistant person in terms of the mastery and attachment skills necessary for managing the stress of life that you are encountering.

Table 1

Health Profile Summary Sheet

1. Biological Limitations (if any): _____

_____

2. Life Stress: Chronic Illnesses (if any): _____

_____

       Major Life Events (Questionnaire #1): _____

_____

       Hassles (Questionnaire #2): _____

_____

3. Coping Resources—Reasonable Mastery (Questionnaire #3): _____

_____

_____

4. Social Supports—Caring Attachments (Questionnaire #4): _____

_____

* * *

References

Holmes, T. H., and R. H. Rahe. "The Social Readjustment Rating Scale." *Journal of Psychosomatic Research* 2 (1967); 213–18.

Kanner, A. D., J. C. Coyne, C. Schaefer, and R. S. Lazarus. "Comparison of Two Modes of Stress Measurement: Daily Hassles and Uplifts versus Major Life Events." *Journal of Behavioral Medicine* 4 (1981); 1–39.

Rotter, J. B. "Internal Control and External Control: A Sampler." *Psychology Today,* June, 1971, pp. 37–42 and 58–59.

Wilcox, B. L. "Social Support, Life Stress, and Psychological Adjustment: A Test of the Buffering Hypothesis." *American Journal of Community Psychology* 9 (1981); 371–86.

Appendix B: The Project SMART Program

(A Guide for Health Care Professionals who wish to start a Project SMART group)

A Stress-Management Program

A stress-management program has been developed, based on a group treatment model, for persons with general anxiety. Its goals are to (1) reduce somatic arousal and (2) develop more successful coping strategies for common stress events. The basic program utilizes four interventions: (1) a modification of intake of dietary stimulants (caffeine, nicotine, refined white sugar), (2) relaxation exercises, (3) an individualized hard-exercise program, and (4) a stress inoculation process to learn adaptive coping strategies for common stressful situations.

The groups meet for eight 90-minute sessions. Homogeneity of composition and a group size of eight members appear to encourage group interaction and compliance. For participants who are patients, this may be their primary treatment; for many, the stress-management group is an adjunct to their overall treatment plan. For participants who are not patients this approach is usually presented as part of an in-service training program and is adapted to individual organizational needs.

Screening. Applicants are referred to the group by their internist, therapist, or employer. After reviewing each case, the group leader screens potential members for possible psychosis or disabling disturbances. Group members are also apprised of the logistics and parameters of the group, e.g., that active participation is expected. A physical exam is required to rule out any medical problem that could cause anxiety (e.g., hyperthyroid, mitral valve prolapse, etc.), and to certify that members are ready for the hard-exercise component of the program. If a person wishes to participate, he or she is given a medical clearance form to be completed by his or her physician before the first group meeting. An important aspect of the screening is giving the individual the chance to ask questions, thereby enhancing his or her sense of control and participation.

First session. In this initial meeting, participants are asked to give examples of stressful situations and symptoms of anxiety. The common elements of these situations and symptoms are discussed by the group. A brief presentation of the physiology of somatic arousal[20] and the characteristics of stress-resistant people follows. Next, the participants are shown how to take their pulse, are given forms to record their pulse rates three times a day, and are shown how to average them for the next seven days. This average pulse rate is then used as a physiological measure of somatic arousal. Finally, each member is given the following questionnaires to complete before the next session: the Schedule of Recent Experience,[35] a measure of major life events; the Hassles Scale,[36] a measure of ordinary daily frustrating situations; the Taylor Manifest Anxiety Scale;[37] the Beck Depression Inventory,[38] and the locus of Control Orientation Scale,[39] a measure of how much control an individual perceives he or she has over the environment and its reinforcers. The first two of these measures appear to be methodologically weak,[40] and members are so advised.

Second session. This meeting opens with a review of the previous week's theoretical material and a check for compliance with the pulse baseline data. Each participant scores the questionnaires as the group leader reads the correct answers. Each measure is scored in its standardized format, and norms are presented so that each individual will have a clearer understanding of his or her stressors and their impact on current functioning. The four-step stress-management program is presented next. The session closes with each person entering into a behavioral contract[41] to modify one of the three dietary stimulants in some small way.

Third session. This session begins with a brief review of all theoretical material, and checks are made of compliance with pulse recording requirements and adherence to dietary modification. The remainder of this session is spent in training and practicing the relaxation response.[25] Members are taught to sit quietly, breathe deeply and slowly, and to concentrate on an image of a restful place, if they wish. Members are asked to practice this response three times a day for ten minutes each time.

Fourth session. This meeting begins with an assessment of compliance with the assigned tasks. Behavioral contracts are renegotiated for small but increasing reductions in dietary stimulants. The next 15 minutes are used to induce the relaxation response, and the remainder of the session is spent developing a hard-exercise program for each member. Each person is asked to commit himself or herself to three 20-minute periods of some form of hard exercise for the next seven days. Members are taught the importance of starting an exercise program gradually and of following all specific instructions from their physicians. Warm-up and cool-down periods are then explained and modeled[42] to insure good health practices. This session closes with a brisk 15-minute walk.

Sessions five to eight. Each remaining session begins with the necessary checks for compliance. These are followed by a brisk 15-minute walk, and then by 15 minutes of relaxation training. The rest of the time is spent in stress inoculation training.[43] This procedure emphasizes the importance of negative cognitions in inducing anxiety, and the need to develop general adaptive cognitive and behavioral coping strategies. Good cognitive coping techniques include strategies to inhibit negative thinking, to relabel physiological arousal as a signal for positive action, and to provide self-praise. Behavioral strategies include techniques to minimize somatic arousal and direct action to resolve stressful situations. A common group stress inoculation task might be coping with urban rush-hour traffic. Direct courses of action would be discussed (e.g., using less traveled roads, changing time commitments, working flexible hours, using the relaxation response) along with cognitive strategies (altering negative thinking, e.g., thinking "This is not the worst thing that has happened to me; I'll enjoy the baseball game on the radio"). Participants play roles during group time and are encouraged to use these strategies in vivo during the subsequent week. Problems can be common daily hassles, or situations specific to group needs, such as teaching courtroom summation skills to lawyers or supermarket strategies to agoraphobics.

—Flannery, R. B., Jr. Toward Stress-Resistant persons: A stress management approach to the treatment of anxiety. *American Journal of Preventive Medicine* 3 (1987); 25–30.

Appendix C: Relaxation Instructions

I have taught these relaxation exercises to many people. Such exercises are basically right-brain activities. Thus they lower the whole stress response all at once. In addition, you can use these exercises in public or private without anyone knowing; these exercises are portable and you can take them with you; and best of all there is no cost to purchase them other than your own time in learning to use them. If you used these exercises for as little as ten or fifteen minutes a day, you would feel remarkably better in a short period of time.

The exercises that I will present here are an amalgamation of deep breathing (Benson, 1975), release of muscle tension and the use of pleasant imagery. I have taught these exercises to thousands of people over the years, and this appears to be the best combination for the greatest number of people. There are several different types of relaxation exercises available, and you may want to add in some additional exercises that interest you.

In doing these exercises, you will be safe and in control. If a true emergency arose, your mind and body would immediately rise from the relaxation state, and you would be capable of solving the problem. When some people relax, they feel out of control or have unusual thoughts. Persons who have lived through traumatic situations sometimes feel this way. In their minds, being relaxed means not being vigilant and in control. If you have this response to the exercises, stop doing them, and try an aerobic exercise program instead. Aerobic exercise accomplishes similar stress reduction, and you'll feel more in control. If you have lung disease, check with your physician before you begin these exercises.

As I have noted, my relaxation program contains three parts: slow-paced breathing, the cognitive release of muscle tension, and imagining a pleasant and relaxing image.

Let us begin with the breathing. Because of the pace of our daily life, we learn to breathe more quickly than we need to. We can slow down our respiration cycle without any serious side effects. The cycle I use in teaching people runs on five-second intervals. Five seconds to inhale a full breath using the whole lung. Five seconds of holding that air. Five seconds of exhaling the air in a slow steady column. Five seconds of sitting quietly without drawing your next breath. Then the twenty-second cycle begins again. Try it now, if you wish. Like any other skill, learning this will take practice. Go at your own pace, but leave time for each of the four intervals, and go more slowly than you normally would. (If you are a smoker, you will have more difficulty with these exercises). Five seconds: inhale. Five seconds: hold. Five seconds: exhale. Five seconds: hold. Then begin again.

The second part of these exercises includes the release of muscle tension in the muscle groups listed below. Our minds are remarkably powerful instruments for coping with stress. If you think of your muscles being released of tension or set free, your brain will in fact release the muscle tension. When you are breathing slowly as outlined above, then think of the various muscles in your body to be freed of tension. Think of them being released, and they will be. For example, inhale, hold (release the muscle tension in your toes, arches, and heels), exhale, hold. Inhale, hold (release the muscle tension in your ankles, shins, and knees), exhale, hold, and so forth.

Below is a list of the muscle clusters that I teach to others. Do one grouping at a time, and remember to maintain your slower breathing pace.

1. Toes, arches, and heels;
2. Ankles, shins, and knees;
3. Thighs, buttocks, and anal sphincter;
4. Lower back, up the back to the neck and shoulders;
5. Abdomen, chest muscles, again up to the neck and shoulders;
6. Upper arms, forearms, down to the wrists;
7. Each hand, each finger, each fingertip;
8. The muscles in each shoulder and all around the base of the neck;
9. The whole neck, the tongue, and the jaw;

10. The dental cavity, the mouth muscles, and the upper facial cheeks;
11. The eye muscles, the forehead, and the top and back of the scalp.

Breathe slowly, and go through each muscle grouping—one grouping per respiration cycle. You can complete these two parts of the relaxation exercise in about ten to fifteen minutes after you have had a chance to practice.

The third component of my approach is the addition of a pleasant and relaxing image. Think of some place you have been that was pleasant or some place that you would like to visit. Make sure the place you choose has no unpleasant memories for you. Do not select that secluded beach where you broke up with your sweetheart, do not select that breathtaking mountain where you broke your leg skiing. Make sure your choice is truly pleasant for you.

After you are breathing slowly and rhythmically, and have released all the muscle tension in your body, close your eyes and imagine your special place. Make your image as real as if you were actually there. Whatever you might see or taste or touch or smell if you were really there—be sure to include those things in your image. If your image is unclear, or if you have trouble thinking in images, picture yourself floating on a cloud of your favorite color, or picture yourself sitting before a curtain blowing in the summer breezes. Imagine your pleasant scene for five minutes. Be sure you continue to breathe slowly, and keep all the muscle tension in your body released. Relax.

With a little practice, these relaxation exercises of breathing slowly, releasing muscle tension, and imagining a relaxing place can be quite effective in reducing our stress response. If you have a particularly stressful day, you can do them for ten minutes in the morning, ten minutes at noon, ten minutes at suppertime, and ten minutes before bedtime. These exercises have the added advantage of being flexible. If you are anticipating an event that is making you anxious, these exercises can help beforehand. You can also use them when the event is over to return your body to its normal stress-free resting state. These exercise components take practice, but they are very helpful in reducing the negative fallout from life stress.

Appendix D

General Instructions for Aerobic Exercise

(1) See your physician to obtain medical clearance before you begin an aerobic exercise program, and always comply with any suggestions or limitations that your physician may give you.

(2) Your aerobic exercises should begin with a three to five minute warm-up period. Slowly walk, or jog or run in place. Bend, stretch, twist, and generally limber up your body. The warm-up period loosens muscles and joints, increases circulation, and helps to prevent injury. Stretch passively your major muscle groups. For those with greater interest specific diagrammed warm-up stretch exercises may be found in the two references listed below.

(3) Now begin your aerobic exercise. Be sure that you have chosen an exercise that is fun for you to do so that you will be motivated to continue. Start in small, gradual and manageable steps. *Stop if you feel faint, pain, or shortness of breath.* A healthful exercise goal to work towards is three twenty-minute periods of such exercise on three different days in any one calendar week.

(4) Finish with a cool-down period when you have completed your aerobics. The cool-down period is similar to the warm-up period. Again, for three to five minutes walk about slowly, or jog or run in place slowly. Also do some mild stretching for specific muscle groups. The cool-down period allows your body to adjust from intense exercise to its more normal resting pace.

References

Greenberg, J. S. *Comprehensive Stress Management.* (2nd Ed.) Dubuque, Iowa: William Brown Publishers, 1986, pp. 206–7.

Johnson, S. B. *Walking Handbook.* Dallas, TX: Institute for Aerobics Research, 1989, pp. 26–27.

Selected Readings

The following list contains selected readings for the materials presented in each chapter to enable the reader to explore various issues of interest in greater depth. Most of the readings have additional bibliographies of their own.

Chapter One: Stress-Resistant Persons: Reasonable Mastery

Allen, R. F. *Lifegain* with Shirley Linde. New York: Appleton Century Crofts, 1981.

Flannery, R. B., Jr. Towards stress-resistant persons: A stress management approach in the treatment of anxiety. *American Journal of Preventive Medicine* 3 (1987a); 25–30.

Hennig, M., and A. Jardin. *The Managerial Woman.* Garden City: Anchor Press/Doubleday, 1977.

Hinkle, L. E., Jr., and H. G. Wolfe. "Ecological Investigations of the Relationship between Illness, Life Experiences, and the Social Environment." *Annals of Internal Medicine* 49 (1958); 1373–78.

Levinson, D. *The Seasons of a Man's Life.* New York: Knopf, 1978.

Maddi, S. R., and S. C. Kobassa. *The Hardy Executive: Health Under Stress.* Homewood, Illinois: Dow-Jones-Irwin, 1984.

Maslow, A. *Toward a Psychology of Being.* Princeton: Van Nostrand, 1968.

Scitovsky, T. *The Joyless Economy: An Inquiry into Human Satisfaction and Consumer Dissatisfaction.* London: Oxford University Press, 1976.

Vaillant, G. *Adaptation to Life.* Boston: Little, Brown, 1977.

White, R. W. "Motivation Reconsidered: The Concept of Competence." *Psychological Review* 66 (1959); 279–333.

Chapter Two: Stress-Resistant Persons: Caring Human Attachments

Beutler, L. E., D. Engle, M. E. Oro-Beutler, R. Doldrup, and K. Meredith. "Inability to Express Intense Affect: A Common Link Between Depression and Pain." *Journal of Consulting and Clinical Psychology* 54 (1986) 752–59.

Bowlby, J. *Attachment and Loss.* Vol. 1: *Attachment:* New York: Basic Books, 1969.

Engle, G. E. "Sudden and Rapid Death During Psychological Stress: Folklore or Folk Wisdom?" *Annals of Internal Medicine* 74 (1971) 771–82.

Flannery, R. B., Jr. "Social Support and Psychological Trauma: A Methodological Review." *Journal of Traumatic Stress* 3 (1990) 593–611.

House, J. S., K. R. Landis, and D. Umberson "Social Relationships and Health." *Science* 241 (1988) 540–44.

Kiecolt-Glasser, J. K., and R. Glasser "Psychosocial Moderators of Immune Function." *Annals of Behavioral Medicine* 9 (1986); 3–10.

Kubler-Ross, E. *On Death and Dying*. New York: Macmillan, 1969.

Lynch, J. J. *The Broken Heart: The Medical Consequences of Loneliness*. New York: Basic Books, 1977.

Lynch, J. J. *The Language of the Heart: The Body's Response to Human Dialogue*. New York: Basic Books, 1985.

Weisman, A., and T. Hackett "Predilection to Death." *Psychosomatic Medicine* 23 (1961); 232–56.

Chapter Three: Stress and Burnout: When Mastery and Attachment Fail

Albee, G. A competency model to replace the defect model. In ed. M. S. Gibbs, J. R. Lackenmeyer, and J. Segal, pp. 213–38. *Community Psychology: Theoretical and Empirical Approaches*. New York: Gardner Press, 1980.

Asterita, M. F. *The Physiology of Stress, with Special Reference to the Neuroendocrine System*. New York: Human Sciences Press, 1985.

Barnett, R., L. Biener, and G. K. Baruch, eds. *Gender and Stress*. New York: Free Press, 1987.

Cannon, W. *The Wisdom of the Body*. New York: Norton, 1963.

Cox, T. *Stress*. Baltimore: University Park Press, 1978.

Dohrenwend, B., and B. Dohrenwend, eds. *Stressful Life Events: Their Nature and Effects*. New York: Wiley, 1974.

Lazarus, R. S., and S. Folkman, *Stress, Appraisal, and Coping*. New York: Springer, 1984.

Maslach, C. *Burnout: The Cost of Caring*. Englewood Cliffs, NJ: Prentice-Hall, 1982.

Selye, H. *The Stress of Life*. New York: McGraw-Hill, 1956.

Simeons, A. *Man's Presumptuous Brain: An Evolutionary Interpretation of Psychosomatic Disease*. New York: Dutton, 1960.

Chapter Four: The Rat Race: The Cultural Sources of Stress

Bailyn, B. *The Peopling of British North America: An Introduction*. New York: Knopf, 1986.

Barnett, R., and R. Muller *Global Reach: The Power of Multinational Corporations*. New York: Simon and Schuster, 1974.

Bell, D. *The Cultural Contradictions of Capitalism*. New York: Basic Books, 1976.

Boorstin, D. J. *The Republic of Technology: Reflections on Our Future Community*. New York: Harper and Row, 1978.

Easton, S., M. Shostak, and M. Konner *The Paleolithic Prescription: A Program of Diet and Exercise, and a Design for Living*. New York: Harper and Row, 1988.

Heilbroner, R. *The Future as History: The Historic Currents of Our Time and the Direction in Which They Are Taking America*. New York: Harper Torchbooks, 1968.

Lasch, C. *The Culture of Narcissism: American Life in an Age of Diminishing Expectations*. New York: Norton, 1978.

Sagan, L. N. *The Health of Nations: True Causes of Sickness and Well-being.* New York: Basic Books, 1987.

Sorokin, P. A. *The Crisis of Our Age: The Social and Cultural Outlook.* New York: Dutton, 1941.

Weber, M. *The Protestant Ethic and the Spirit of Capitalism.* Trans. by T. Parsons. New York: Scribner's Sons, 1958.

Chapter Five: Illness: The Peril of Ignoring Stress

Brenner, H. M. *Economy and Mental Health.* Baltimore: Johns Hopkins, 1973.

Charlesworth, E. A., and R. G. Nathan *Stress Management: A Comprehensive Guide to Wellness.* New York: Atheneum, 1984.

Dawber, T. *The Framingham Study: The Epidemiology of Atherosclerotic Disease.* Cambridge, MA: Harvard University Press, 1980.

Friedman, M., and R. Rosenman *Type A Behavior and Your Heart.* New York: Knopf, 1974.

Justice, B. *Who Gets Sick: How Beliefs, Moods, and Thoughts Affect Your Health.* Los Angeles: J. P. Tarcher, 1988.

Khantzian, E. "The Self-Medication Hypothesis of Addictive Disorders: Focus on Heroin and Cocaine Dependence." *American Journal of Psychiatry,* 142 (1985); 1259–64.

Riesman, D. *The Lonely Crowd: A Study of the Changing American Character.* New Haven: Yale University Press, 1950.

Tavris, C. *Anger: The Misunderstood Emotion.* New York: Simon and Schuster, 1982.

van der Kolk, B. A., ed. *Psychological Trauma.* Washington, DC: American Psychiatric Press, 1987.

Zinberg, N. *Drug, Set, and Setting: The Basis for Controlled Intoxicant Use.* New Haven: Yale University Press, 1984.

Chapter Six: Mastery: Your Life-style and Project SMART

Belloc, N., and L. Breslow "Relationship of Physical Health Status and Health Practices." *Preventive Medicine* 1 (1972); 409–21.

Benson, H. *The Relaxation Response.* New York: Morrow, 1975.

Brickman, P. *Commitment, Conflict and Caring.* Edited by C. B. Wortman and R. Sorrentino. Englewood Cliffs, New Jersey: Prentice-Hall, Inc., 1987.

Brody, J. *Jane Brody's Nutrition Book: A Lifetime Guide to Good Eating for Better Health and Weight Control.* New York: Norton, 1981.

Cooper, K. H. *Aerobics.* New York: Bantam Books, 1968.

DeGrazia, S. *Of Time, Work, and Leisure.* New York: Anchor, 1964.

Farquhar, J. *The American Way of Life Need Not Be Hazardous to Your Health.* New York: Norton, 1978.

Linder, S. *The Harried Leisure Class.* New York: Columbia University Press, 1970.

Meichenbaum, D. *Cognitive-Behavior Modification: An Integrative Approach.* New York: Plenum, 1977.

Packard, V. *A Nation of Strangers.* New York: Pocket Books, 1974.

Chapter Seven: Mastery: Financial Decisions

Boorstin, D. *The Image; or, What Happened to the American Dream.* New York: Atheneum, 1962.

Cherniss, C. *Staff Burnout: Job Stress in the Human Services.* Beverly Hills: Sage, 1980.

Engel, L., and P. Wycoff *How to Buy Stocks.* Boston: Little Brown, 1976.

Fabe, M., and N. Wikler *Up against the Clock: Career Women Speak on the Choice to Have Children.* New York: Random House, 1979.

Harragan, B. C. *Games Mother Never Taught You: Corporate Gamesmanship for Women.* New York: Rawson, 1977.

Levinson, H. *Psychological Man.* Cambridge, MA: The Levinson Institute, 1976.

Packard, V. *The Status Seekers: An Exploration of Class Behavior in America and the Hidden Barriers That Affect You, Your Community, Your Future.* New York: McKay, 1959.

Porter, S. *Sylvia Porter's Money Book: How to Earn It, Spend It, Save It, Invest It, Borrow It and Use It to Better Your Life.* Garden City, NY: Doubleday, 1975.

Steele, A. *Upward Nobility: How to Win the Rat Race without Becoming a Rat.* New York: Times Books, 1978.

Watkins, A. *Building or Buying the High-Quality House at the Lowest Cost.* New York: Dolphin, 1962.

Chapter Eight: Attachment: Making Relationships Work

Bennis, W., and P. Slater *The Temporary Society.* New York: Harper and Row, 1968.

Hall, F., and D. Hall *The Two Career Couple.* Reading, MA: Addison-Wesley, 1979.

Heller, J. *Something Happened.* New York: Knopf, 1974.

Lederer, W., and D. Jackson *The Mirages of Marriage.* New York: Norton, 1968.

Lewis, C. S. *The Four Loves.* New York: Harcourt, Brace, 1960.

Packard, V. *The Hidden Persuaders.* New York: D. McKay, 1957.

Sager, C., and B. Hunt *Intimate Partners: Hidden Patterns in Love Relationships.* New York: McGraw-Hill, 1979.

Schor, J. B. *The Overworked American: The Unexpected Decline of Leisure.* New York: Basic Books, 1991.

Steinbeck, J. *East of Eden.* New York: Bantam, 1952.

Updike, J. *Couples.* New York: Knopf, 1968.

Chapter Nine: Mastery and Attachment: The Special Problem of Learned Helplessness

Bandura, A. "Self-Efficacy: Towards a Unifying Theory of Behavioral Change." *Psychological Review* 84 (1977); 191–215.

Flannery, R. B., Jr. "From Victim to Survivor: A Stress Management Approach in the Treatment of Learned Helplessness. In *Psychological Trauma*, ed. B. A. van der Kolk, pp. 217–32. Washington, DC: American Psychiatric Press, 1987b.

Garber, J., and M. E. P. Seligman, eds. *Human Helplessness: Theory and Application.* San Francisco: Freeman, 1975.

Herman, J. L. *Father-Daughter Incest.* Cambridge, MA: Harvard University Press, 1981.

Horowitz, M. *Stress Response Syndromes.* New York: Aronson, 1976.

Janoff-Bulman, R. "The Aftermath of Victimization: Rebuilding Shattered Assumptions." In *Trauma and Its Wake: The Study and Treatment of Post-Traumatic Stress Disorder,* ed. C. R. Figley, pp. 15–35, New York: Brunner/Mazel, 1985.

Koss, M., and M. Harvey *The Rape Victim: Clinical and Community Approaches to Treatment.* Lexington, MA: Stephen Greene Press, 1987.

Lavelle, J., and R. Mollica, "Southeast Asian refugees." In *Clinical Guidelines in Cross-Cultural Mental Health,* ed. L. Comaz-Dias and E. E. Griffith, pp. 262–304. New York: Wiley and Sons, 1985.

Lindemann, E. "Symptomatology and Management of Acute Grief." *American Journal of Psychiatry* 101 (1944); 141–48.

Seligman, M. E. P. *Helplessness: On Depression, Development, and Death.* New York: W. H. Freeman, 1975.

Chapter Ten: Mastery and Attachment: Love of Self and Others

Antonovsky, A. *Health, Stress and Coping.* San Francisco: Jossey-Bass, 1979.

Antonovsky, A. *Unraveling the Mystery of Health: How People Manage Stress and Stay Well.* San Francisco: Jossey-Bass, 1987.

Beck, A. T. *Depression: Causes and Treatment.* Philadelphia: University of Pennsylvania Press, 1970.

Durant, W., and A. Durant *The Lessons of History.* New York: Simon and Schuster, 1968.

Ellis, A. *Rational-Emotive Psychotherapy.* New York: Stuart, 1963.

Erikson, E. H. *Childhood and Society.* New York: Norton, 1963.

Peck, M. *People of the Lie: The Hope for Healing Human Evil.* New York: Simon and Schuster, 1983.

Peplau, A. L., and D. Pearlman eds. *Loneliness: A Sourcebook of Current Theory, Research, and Therapy.* New York: Wiley-Interscience, 1982.

Plumb, J. *The Death of the Past.* Boston: Houghton-Mifflin, 1970.

Teilhard de Chardin, P. *The Phenomenon of Man.* New York: Harper-Row, 1959.

Acknowledgements

The author and publisher gratefully acknowledge permission from the following sources to reprint material in this book:

Plenum Publishing Corporation for permission to reprint The Hassles Scale, "Comparison of Two Modes of Stress Measurement: Daily Hassles and Uplifts Versus Major Life Events," by A. Kanner, A.D. Coyne, C. Schaefer, and R.S. Lazarus in *Journal of Behavioral Medicine,* 4 (1981).

Human Resources Institute, Inc., Burlington, Vermont, for permission to reprint "The Life Expectancy Quiz," which appeared in *Lifeagain* by Robert F. Allen with Shirley Linde.

The Saturday Evening Post, for permission to reprint the following cartoons. "I found the bullets," "Do you want to talk about it?," "I'm ready dear!," "I thought you might be looking for this. The garage door has been going up and down for the past ten minutes," "No, Gorko, no junk food," "Lemonade 5¢ Now sugar free," "Will you stop referring to our anniversaries as rounds?" Reprinted with permission of *The Saturday Evening Post,* ©1944 (Renewed), BFL & MS, Inc., Indianapolis, Indiana.

American Psychiatric Publishing, Inc. (www.appi.org) for permission to reprint "Comparison of Coping Strategies" table by R.B. Flannery, Jr., "From Victim to Survivor: A Stress Management Approach in the Treatment of Learned Helplessness," in *Psychological Trauma,* edited by B.A. van der Kolk, American Psychiatric Press, Washington, DC, p. 221 (1987).

Mother Jones for permission to reprint "I find you up in the middle of winter and you tell me nothing's wrong?" drawing ©1981 by Michael Maslin.

Elsevier Science for permission to reprint T.H. Holmes and R.H. Rahe, "The Social Readjustment Rating Scale," *Journal of Psychosomatic Research, 11,* 213-218 (1967).

Julian B. Rotter and *Psychology Today* for permission to reprint "Internal Control-External Control: A Sampler," from *Psychology Today* (1971) by Sussex Publishers, Inc.

Brian L. Wilcox, Ph.D., University of Nebraska, Lincoln, Nebraska, for permission to reprint "The Social Support Index" (Third Revision).

Elsevier Science for permission to reprint "Toward Stress-Resistant Persons: A Stress Management Approach to the Treatment of Anxiety" by Raymond B. Flannery, Jr., *American Journal of Preventive Medicine, 3* (1), 26-27 (1987).

About the Author

Raymond B. Flannery, Jr., Ph.D., a licensed clinical psychologist, is Associate Clinical Professor of Psychology, Department of Psychiatry, Harvard Medical School and Adjunct Assistant Professor of Psychiatry, Department of Psychiatry, The University of Massachusetts Medical School. A nationally recognized expert, Dr. Flannery has lectured extensively in Canada, Europe, and the United States and is the author of six books and over 100 peer-reviewed articles in medical and scientific journals on the topics of stress, violence, and victimization. His work has been translated into four foreign languages.

Dr. Flannery and his wife life in the suburbs of Boston.

INDEX

Absenteeism, 92
Acceptance, importance of, 52
Accidents, 56, 92, 106
   See also Motor vehicle accidents
Acute/protest phase, of PTSD, 151–52
Addison's disease, 91
Adrenalin, 63, 66
Aerobic exercise, 26, 28, 68, 91, 110,
   115, 116, 117
   and hunter/gatherers, 75
Affairs, 136, 146–47
Agoraphobia, 91
Agricultural/farmers, 76–78, 85, 86
AIDS, 43
Albee, Dr. George, 59, 60, 86
Alcoholism, 56, 91–92, 93, 95, 97,
   98–100, 101, 106, 107–8, 145,
   156
Allen, Dr. Robert F., 30, 32
American Dream, 57–58
Amphetamines, 91, 100, 101
Anger, 52, 100, 101
   See also Rage
"Anniversary death," 94–95
Antonovsky, Aaron, 171
Anxiety, 56, 101
   See also Separation anxiety
Aristotle, 21
Arthritis, 30, 91, 145, 162–63
Asthma, 98
Atherosclerosis, 82, 106

Bailyn, Bernard, 77
Barbiturates, 100, 101
Bargaining, 52
Beck, Dr. Aaron, 165–66
Behavior, 49–50, 97
   and technology, 82–84
   See also Driver behavior
Belloc, Dr. Nedra, 106
Biological limitations, 30, 59

Bonding, and marriage, 143
Boorstin, Daniel, 77, 78
Boredom, 27
Bowlby, Dr. John, 40, 147
Brain injuries, 99
Breakfast, 109
Brenner, Dr. M. Harvey, 93
Breslow, Dr. Lester, 106
Buffers, 48–49
Burnout, 63, 67, 114–15

Caffeine, 27, 28, 108, 116
Cancer, 56, 82, 95, 99, 106, 110
   See also Colon cancer; Lung cancer
Cardiac system, 41–43
Career choice, 92
Caring attachments, 37–53, 86–88,
   101, 163–64, 167, 175
   basics of, 49–52
   and burnout, 115
   and heart disease, 94–95
   and hunter/gatherers, 75
   and learned helplessness, 155–56
   nature of, 39–41
   and physiology, 41–44
   and psychology, 44–49
   and stress-resistant people, 147–48
   See also Relationships
Cash reserves, 134
Charlesworth, Dr. Edward, 91
Cherniss, C., 124
Children, 56, 130, 131–32, 145
Cholesterol, 94, 108
Chronic/numbing phase, of PTSD,
   152–53
Cigarettes. *See* Smoking
Circadian rhythm, 63, 64, 65
Cirrhosis of liver, 82, 99, 106
Cocaine, 101
Cognitive appraisal, 63
Cognitive evaluation, 65